Rabindranath Tagore, the Nobel Prize for Literature in 1913 & the British Raj

To order additional copies of this book, contact
Toll Free 800 101 2657 (Singapore)
Toll Free 1 800 81 7340 (Malaysia)
orders.singapore@partridgepublishing.com

www.partridgepublishing.com/singapore

Rabindranath Tagore, the Nobel Prize for Literature in 1913 & the British Raj: Some Untold Stories

[Also containing the full text of his Nobel Prize winning book Gitanjali (Song Offerings) in English version with an Introduction by W. B. Yeats]

By

A. B. M. Shamsud Doulah

PARTRIDGE
A Penguin Random House Company

To:

The loving memory of my esteemed father
Late M. A. Rahman of Village: Jashilda, Vikrampur, District:
Dhaka; Formerly: Assistant Editor of ***The Hindustan Times***,
New Delhi; Editor, ***The Renaissance of Islam***, Calcutta; & ***The
Nation***, Calcutta, later on which was transferred to his friend Sarat
Chandra Bose, Member of Central Committee of All-India National
Congress and the elder brother of India's greatest Freedom Fighter
against the British Raj in India *Netaji* Subhas Chandra Bose.

Rabindranath Tagore in 1913

Contents

Preface xi

Chapter 1   Some Introductory Notes... 1
Chapter 2   British occupation of India and patronage to non- Muslims ... 16
Chapter 3   Rabindranath Tagore followed the foot-steps of
             Raja Ram Mohan Roy and such others................................ 20
Chapter 4   The influence of *Prince* Dwarakanath Tagore....................23
Chapter 5   The influence of Kalidas, Lalon Fakir and D. L. Roy etc....... 26
Chapter 6   'Terrorist movement' in Bengal.. 28
Chapter 7   British colonial rulers'
             continued patronage of the elite non-Muslims 30
Chapter 8   Shifting of capital from Calcutta to New Delhi....................33
Chapter 9   Brahmo Samaj & Tagore 37
Chapter 10   Rabindranath Tagore's Western and Jewish contacts.............39
Chapter 11   The Nobel Prize for Literature in 1913 43
Chapter 12   Rabindranath Tagore was awarded Nobel Prize as an
             'Anglo-Indian' poet...50
Chapter 13   Why Rabindranath Tagore was not present for
             receiving the Nobel Prize?..65
Chapter 14   Rabindranath Tagore in the 21st century...............................72
Chapter 15   Epilogue 75

A Select Bibliography on Rabindranath Tagore 77
Appendix 79
Index..135

Preface

1. The roots of British colonial rule in the Indian sub-continent were planted deep by London against the will of the people of the region.

2. In 1947 the British Governor-General Lord Mountbatten perpetuated a 'divide and rule policy' through partition of the then India. He partitioned the united India, under a London plan, creating New Delhi administered India of today having majority Hindu population; and Karachi administered Pakistan having majority Muslim population in two distant locations, as such came to be known as East Pakistan and West Pakistan. Subsequently, West Pakistan became today's Islamabad administered Pakistan and in 1971, being alienated by a Liberation War against the colonial rule of Islamabad, East Pakistan became Dhaka administered independent Bangladesh.

3. Delhi administered India decided to adopt Hindi as the state language of India. It is notable that Rabindranath Tagore always supported the adoption of Hindi as an All-India language.

4. *Netaji* Subhas Chandra Bose and *Bangabandhu* Sheikh Mujibur Rahman were two great Bengalee political leaders. *Netaji* Subhas Chandra Bose was always opposed to the colonial rule of the Britishers in India and *Bangabandhu* Sheikh Mujibur Rahman was opposed to the colonial rule of the then (West) Pakistan, which imposed Urdu as the only state language for both East and West Pakistan, and enforced a ruthless undemocratic rule in fully Bengali-speaking East Pakistan, leading to the emergence of independent Bangladesh.

5. Considering the background of undemocratic colonial rule of the Britishers, this book is presented, with various relevant references, for the convenience of the readers.

6. The British rulers in India always had a distaste and inner hatred towards the Bengalees in general. The following words of Thomas Babington Macaulay in his famous essay on Lord Robert Clive reflect it:

> Whatever the Bengalee does he does languidly. His favourite pursuits are sedentary. He shrinks from bodily exertion; and, though voluble in dispute, and singularly pertinacious in the war of chicane, he seldom engages in a personal conflict, and scarcely ever enlists as a soldier. We doubt whether there be a hundred genuine Bengalees in the whole army of the East India Company. There never, perhaps, existed a people so thoroughly fitted by nature and by habit for a foreign yoke *["yoke" meaning 'rule' here– Ed.].*

> (From *Critical and Historical Essays*. Vol. I by Thomas Babington Macaulay, London).

> [NOTE: Thomas Babington Macaulay the compiler of the above referred essay on Lord Clive is as important to the Indians as is his infamous *Indian Penal Code* (unchanged) which still rules India, Pakistan and Bangladesh. It was written in 1833 and implemented in 1861 by the British Raj. This is noted from the notes of the editor of the above work entitled: *Critical and Historical Essays*. Vol. I by Thomas Babington Macaulay, London].

> *See:* http://mrtpix.tripod.com/clive.pdf

This is to request the readers to understand the people by 'Bengalee' and the language by 'Bengali', noting the spellings. Currently the words are used wrongly by many.

7. The capital of the British Raj was subsequently shifted from Calcutta to New Delhi in 1911. Most of the notable administrative buildings of today's Indian capital New Delhi were built during the British Raj before the Second World War.

8. During the last few years I wrote from time to time several short articles in several newspapers and in various Internet *blogs* about the decline in Rabindranath Tagore's popularity, in spite of massive official publicity and patronage, especially in India and Bangladesh. Many readers criticized my observations and many agreed with my views.

9. While responding, either favourably or unfavourably, everybody wanted to see the supporting documentations or references, which could not be possible to be furnished for many reasons, including the possibility copyright infringements. As a matter of fact the subject of declining popularity of Rabindranath Tagore, even in India and Bangladesh, is very important in the face of too much propaganda as to his works, thoughts and opinions.

10. In consideration of such a situation, I felt the necessity of publishing this book with various supporting documentations, including one response from Carola Hermelin, Assistant to the Secretary of the Nobel Committee of the Swedish Academy of Stockholm, who awards the Nobel Prize for Literature.

11. The religion Hinduism of today is a cumulated way of living with polytheistic worshipping of various idols, ghosts, animals and trees etc. within the traditional taboos prescribed by the ancient immigrants, known as 'Aryans', to the northern India and Pakistan of today. Nearly all 'Aryans' entered into India through Afghanistan and many of them were from the Middle-Eastern and Central Asian countries.

12. Subsequently they became widespread throughout South Asia. Today they are known as Brahmin (Brahman) Hindus and their religious scriptures are based on the scholarly oral books known as *Vedas, Puranas* and *Upanishads*, etc. supplemented much later by the famous epic poems called *Ramayana* and *Mahabharata*. Earlier these scriptures were in Sanskrit. Until the Middle Ages these were in oral forms. Written translations of these books, even in the Indian languages, came up during the British Raj in India.

13. Later on the above two epic poems were given the written forms by different writers in the names of *Ramayana* and *Mahabharata*. Both the epic poems are having some similarities with Homer's *Iliad* and *Odyssey*.

14. True, many of the 'Aryans' entered the Ancient India from the western and central Asian countries mostly through Afghanistan and became settled in today's Northern India and upper Pakistan.

15. We are still not sure if the religious sacred books of the Hindus, including the epics *Ramayana* and *Mahabharata* were written / composed under the influence and impact of the ancient Greek legends and also Homer's *Iliad* and *Odyssey*. But there are many resemblances between the ancient Greek gods and goddesses and the same of the Hindus.

16. The impact and influence of the above Hindu religious scriptures greatly influenced Kalidas and Rabindranath Tagore and many other Bengali Hindu writers like Michael Madhusudan Datta (who was converted into Christianity), *Raja* Ram Mohan Roy, Ishwar Chandra Vidyasagar, and Bankim Chandra Chatterjee etc.

17. Rabindranath Tagore was a Hindu mystic poet, deeply influenced by the pantheistic spiritual values of the great fictional epics *Ramayana* and *Mahabharata* and some of the other ancient Hindu religious books, especially *Upanishads*. He grew under the impact and influence of the Christian and Islamic literatures and cultures.

18. None can deny that Rabindranath Tagore also borrowed from English and Persian literatures. Considering all these facts, I tried to furnish the respective references for the convenience of the readers, towards a better and quick understanding.

19. When, as a student, I attended my classes in the Department of English of the Calcutta University in the years 1962 to 1965, including the Presidency College, I came in contact with the famous Bengalee writers and Rabindranath Tagore specialists like Professor Bishnu Dey, Professor Buddhadev Bose, Professor Khudiram Das, Professor Haraprasad Mitra, Professor Dr. Amalendu Bose, Professor T. N. Sen, and, above all, Professor Dr. Nihar Ranjan Roy and that helped me to be better acquainted with the works of Rabindranath Tagore and his beautiful songs (widely known in Bengali as *Rabindra Sangeet*). But today I find a growing decline in the popularity of Tagore literature. One example, though surprising, I learnt from several final year students, studying

in the Master's degree classes of the Bengali language and literature of Calcutta and Dhaka Universities that they never read *Gitanjali (Song Offerings)*, which is considered to be one of the greatest shining star books of the Bengali literature. In the middle of the 20th Century the situation was not like this.

20. This book is meant for the readers who are interested to know about the cunning passages and mysterious avenues of the Nobel Prize (with reference to its award to Rabindranath Tagore in 1913) which was founded and patronized by Jewish scientist Alfred Nobel.

21. There are some unanswered questions about Rabindranath Tagore's connections with the influential Jews of England and other European countries and also of the United States. We know very little about the poet's contacts with the Swedish Academy. I have tried to give some information, as far as I could hurriedly obtain.

22. Today, Internet is the greatest source of information in the 21st Century and, as such, I have also depended on the Internet references.

23. On random calculations, at present, there are about 350 million Bengalees living in the world, being distributed in Bangladesh; West Bengal, Jharkhand, Bihar, Orissa, Tripura and Assam states etc. of India; and in the other parts of the world. About 60% of them are in Bangladesh; 30% are in West Bengal, Assam, Tripura, Jharkhand and Bihar provinces of India; and about 10% are scattered in various parts of Indian states, Pakistan, United States, United Kingdom, Middle-East and other countries of the world. Perhaps my random figures are not exactly correct. But this is provided just to give an approximate idea.

24. But as the Bengalees are not having high rate of reading habit, the Bengali books and periodicals are not circulated high in number. Though there are more Bengali speaking readers in Calcutta, yet we find comparatively smaller number of readers. Moreover, due to socio-cultural gaps Calcutta has turned into an 'island city' in the sense that very few Bengalee residents keep contacts with the countryside Bengalees in India. On the other hand the Bengali language readers are fast growing in Dhaka. This may be due to population change in these two cities.

25. The above figures are based on my random survey on the basis of scattered reports and statistics. During the last fifty years or more there has not been any official survey of the world Bengali language readership. We hope that there will be some such survey in future.

26. This is a compact book on the subject. If it is written with comprehensive details then this could be done in more than one thousand pages. But I do not think that there is any such necessity in the popularity declining phase of Rabindranath Tagore's writings.

27. Due to work pressure as a lawyer, I could not give much time for undertaking wider research on the subject.

28. With the closer first-hand studies, though scattered, for more than 50 years through reading the literary writings of the poet, his beautiful songs, various writings about him both in Bengali and in English, and by meeting the poet's relations and associates, I have precisely presented my experience on the subject in the following pages.

29. This is neither a complete and exhaustive book, nor a comprehensive treatise on the subject. Such an attempt could make the book ten times voluminous in size. I have tried to make the book a compact and simple one just for the easy understanding of the subject. Keeping such point in mind I have appended all the references. This system of quick respective references help the readers to grasp the meaning and contents of the subject-matter in a more simple and easy way.

30. This is a dictated book. One of my young law associates at my law office in Dhaka, Mr. Aniruddha Sarkar took my dictation from time to time for the making and shaping of this book. I gratefully acknowledge his services.

31. Many of the quotations and references given in this book are taken from the Internet. There are some spelling errors in the quotations and references. But for exactness and authenticity, I have not made any changes by way

of corrections. The websites and blogs mentioned after the quotations and references may be found in original in the Internet.

A.B.M. Shamsud Doulah

MA(Calcutta); MA,LLB(Dhaka), MLS(Hawaii)
Advocate, Supreme Court of Bangladesh
Life Member, Bengali Academy, Dhaka
Formerly: Assistant Professor,
Jagannath College, Dhaka &
Fellow, Royal Society of Arts, London

Victoria Hotel
Singapore
February 19, 2015

Chapter 1

Some Introductory Notes

1. Literature and publicity are well known to be very much inter-related. The most widely read books do not always reflect the fact as to its quality and standard. Germany's Adolf Hitler wrote *Mein Kampf*. It is, perhaps one of the most widely read books in the world, by circulation. It was sold and distributed in several million copies, especially due to the publicity made by Hitler's Minister of Propaganda Joseph Goebbels. But the intrinsic value of the book has greatly evaporated after the Second World War and, therefore, brought the book into a low circulation today and is read by very few readers.

2. In addition, during our time we all know about the "best seller publicity" for books in the United States of America. Many readers buy such books just by seeing such titles in the best seller listings in different periodicals.

3. Rabindranath Tagore is the most well known writer in the Bengali language. But very few of his readers do not deeply observe the nature of his popularity, how it grew. This book is a partial attempt to explain how significant is the role of Nobel Prize in his growing popularity both in Bengal and abroad.

4. The volume of Rabindranath Tagore's literary publications is quite big. His writings have been so far published containing more than 20 volumes, each containing about 800 to 1000 pages. But most of his quality writings were written before he was 70 years of age.

5. His writings published until 1912 was not popular even in Bengal. His name is not even mentioned in the famous book entitled: *The History of Bengali Language and Literature* by Dinesh Chandra Sen, which was published in 1912 by the University of Calcutta, containing more than 1000 pages. There is no evidence that Rabindranath Tagore was popular even among the Bengalee readers before his receiving the Nobel Prize for literature in 1913. After his receiving the Nobel Prize his writings were getting more and more popular among the Bengalee readers. It is important that we should examine the following list of all of his vast major writings as given below:

Works in Bengali	
1878	□ *Kabi-Kahini* (The Tale of the Poet : a story in verse)
1880	□ *Bana-phul* (The Flower of the Woods : a story in verse)
1881	□ *Valmiki Pratibha* (The genius of Balmiki : a musical drama) □ *Bhagna-hridaya* (The Broken Heart : a drama in verse) □ *Rudrachanda* (a drama in verse) □ *Europe-prabasir patra* (Letters of a sojourner in Europe)
1882	□ *Sandhya Sangeet* (Evening Songs : a collection of lyrics) □ *Kal Mrigaya* (The Fatal Hunt : a musical drama)
1883	□ *Bouthakuranir Haat* (The young Queen's market : a novel) □ *Prabhat Sangeet* (Morning songs: a collection of lyrics) □ *Vividha Prasanga* (Miscellaneous Topics: a collection of essays)
1884	□ *Prakritir Pratisodh* (Nature's Revenge : a drama in verse) □ *Bhanu Singha Thakurer Padabali* (collection of poems written after Vaishnava poets under the pen name of 'Bhanu Singha') □ *Chhabi O Gaan* (Sketches and Songs : collection of poems) □ *Nalini* (a prose drama) □ *Saisab Sangeet* (Poems of Childhood : a collection of poems)
1885	□ Rammohan Roy (a pamphlet on Rammohan Roy) □ *Alochona* (Discussions : a collection of essays) □ *Rabichhaya* (The shadow of the Sun : a collection of songs)
1886	□ *Kari o Kamal* (Sharps and Flats : a collection of poems)

1887	▫ *Rajarshi* (The Saint King : a novel) ▫ *Chithipatra* (letters)
1888	▫ *Mayar Khela* (a musical drama) ▫ *Samalochona* (Reviews : a collection of essays)
1889	▫ *Raja 0 Rani* (King and Queen : a drama in verse)
1890	▫ *Visarjan* (Sacrifice : a drama) ▫ *Manasi* (The heart's desire: a collection of poems) ▫ *Mantri Abhisek* (a lecture on Lord Cross's India Bill)
1891	▫ *Europe Jatrir Diary* (Diary of a traveller to Europe)
1892	▫ *Chitrangada* (a drama in verse) ▫ *Goray galad* (Wrong at the Start : a comedy) ▫ *Joy parajay* (story)
1893	▫ *Europe Jatrir Diary* Part II ▫ *Ganer Bahi O Valmiki Pratibha* (a collection of songs incorporating *Valmiki Pratibha*)
1894	▫ *Sonar Tari* (The Golden Boat : a collection of poems) ▫ *Chhoto galpo* (collection of 15 short stories) ▫ *Chitrangada O Viday-Abhisap* (*Chitrangada*) ▫ *Vichitra Galpa* (Parts I & II) ▫ *Katha-Chatustaya* (four short stories)
1895	▫ *Chhele-bhulano Chhara* (nursery rhymes) ▫ *Galpa-Dasak* (ten short stories)
1896	▫ *Chitra* (a collection of poems) ▫ *Malini* (a drama) ▫ *Chaitali* (a collection of poems) ▫ *Nadi* (River : a long poem) ▫ *Sanskrita Siksha* Parts I & II (text book)
1897	▫ *Baikunther Khaata* (Manuscripts of Baikuntha : a comedy) ▫ *Pancha Bhut* (Five Elements : a collection of essays)
1899	▫ *Kanika* (a collection of short poems and epigrams)
1900	▫ *Galpoguchha* (a collection of short stories) ▫ *Kshanika* (The Fleeting One : a collection of poems)

	□ *Kalpana* (Imagination : a collection of poems)
	□ *Katha* (Stories : a collection of ballads)
	□ *BrahmaUpanishad* (a religious essay)
	□ *Kahini* (Tales : a collection of drama in verse and long poems)
1901	□ *Galpa* (Stories : part II of Galpaguchha)
	□ *Bangla Kriyapader Taalika* (List of Bengali verbs : text book)
	□ *Aupanishad Brahma* (a religious essay)
	□ *Naivedya* (Offerings : a collection of poems)
	□ *Brahma-mantra* (a religious essay)
1903	□ Chokher Bali (Eyesore : a novel)
	□ Sishu (Child : children poems)
	□ Karmaphal (Nemesis : a story)
1904	□ *Nastaneer* (The Home Spoilt : a novel)
	□ *Chirakumar Sabha* (The Bachelor's Club : a novel, this was later issued separately as *Prajapatir Nirbandha*)
	□ *Ingraji Sopan*, Part I (a text-book)
1905	□ *Baul* (a collection of songs)
	□ *Atmasakti* (a collection of political essays and lectures)
1906	□ *Naukadubi* (The Wreck : a novel)
	□ *Bharatbarsha* (India : a collection of political essays and lectures)
	□ *Rajbhakti* (a political essay)
	□ *Deshnayak* (a political essay)
	□ *Ingraji Sopan*, Part II (a text-book)
	□ *Kheya* (Ferry : a collection of poems)
1907	□ *Adhunik Sahitya* (Modern Literature : a collection of essays)
	□ *Lokasahitya* (Literature of the People : a collection of essays)
	□ *Prachin Sahitya* (Ancient Literature : a collection of essays)
	□ *Sahitya* (Literature : a collection of essays)
	□ *Vichitra Prabandha* (a collection of essays)
	□ *Charitrapuja* (Tributes to Great Lives : a collection of essays)
	□ *Hasya-Kautuk* (humourous sketches)
	□ *Byanga-Kautuk* (satirical sketches)

1908	□ *Mukut* (The Crown : a prose drama)
	□ *Path-O-Patheya* (an essay)
	□ *Raja Praja* (King and his Subjects : a collection of political essays)
	□ *Samuha* (a collection of political essays)
	□ *Swadesh* (My Country : a collection of political and sociological essays)
	□ *Swamaj* (Society : a collection of essays)
	□ *Saradotsav* (Autumn Festival : a drama)
1909	□ *Brahma Sangeet* (a collection of religious songs)
	□ *Vidyasagar-charit* (two essays on Vidyasagar printed before in Charitrapuja)
	□ *Dharma* (Religion : a collection of essays)
	□ *Chayanika* (an anthology of poems)
	□ *Prayaschitta* (Penace : a drama)
	□ *Sabdatattwa* (a collection of papers on Bengali philology)
1910	□ *Raja* (King of the dark chamber : a drama)
	□ *Gora* (a novel)
	□ *Gitanjali* (Song Offerings)
1911	□ *Aatti Galpa* (eight Stories)
1912	□ *Achalayatan* (a drama)
	□ *Dakghar* (Post Office : a drama)
	□ *Galpa Chaariti* (Four Stories)
	□ *Jiban-Smriti* (Reminiscences)
	□ *Chhinnapatra* (Torn Letters)
	□ *Patha Sanchay* (a text-book)
	□ *Dharmasiksha* (an essay)
	□ *Dharmer Adhikar* (an essay)
1914	□ *Utsarga* (Dedication : a collection of poems)
	□ *Gitimalya* (A Garland of songs)
	□ *Gitali* (a collection of poems and songs)
1915	□ *Bichitra Path* (selection for the use of students)
	□ *Kavyagrantha* (ten volumes of poems and dramas)

1916	□ *Ghare Baire* (Home and the World : a novel) □ *Balaka* (The Swan : a collection of poems) □ *Chaturanga* (a novel) □ *Phalguni* (Cycle of Spring : a drama) □ *Sanchaya* (a collection of essays)
1917	□ *Anubad-charcha* (a text-book) □ *Kartar Ichhaye Karmo* (As the Master Wills : a lecture)
1918	□ *Palataka* (The Run-away : stories in verse) □ *Guru* (stage version of *Achalayatan*)
1919	□ *Japan-jatri* (Travels in Japan)
1920	□ *Poila Nombor* (a short story) □ *Arupratan* (stage version of *Raja*)
1921	□ *Barsa-mangal* (Rain Festival) □ *Sikshar Milan* (Meeting of Cultures : a lecture) □ *Rinsodh* (stage version of *Saradotsav*) □ *Satyer Ahovaan* (Call of Truth : a lecture)
1922	□ *Sishu Bholanath* (child poems) □ *Lipika* (Letter : prose-poems) □ *Muktadhara* (Free Current : a drama)
1923	□ *Basanta* (Spring : a musical drama)
1925	□ *Purabi* (a collection of poems) □ *Griha prabesh* (a drama) □ *Sankalan* (a collection of prose) □ *Sesh barshan* (The last shower : a musical drama)
1926	□ *Rakta karabi* (Red Oleanders : a drama) □ *Natir puja* (The dancing girl's worship : a drama) □ *Prabahini* (a collection of songs) □ *Chirakumar sabha* (stage version of *Prajapatir Nirbandha*) □ *Sodh bodh* (All square : a comedy) □ *Lekhon* (Autographs : verses with English translations)
1927	□ *Ritu ranga* (The Play of the Seasons : a musical drama)

1928	▫ *Sesh raksha* (stage version of *Goray galad*) ▫ *Palliprakriti* (address of the anniversary of Sriniketan)
1929	▫ *Sesher Kabita* (Last poem : a novel) ▫ *Mahua* (a collection of poems) ▫ *Tapati* (a drama) ▫ *Jogajog* (a novel) ▫ *Paritran* (stage version of *Prayaschitta*) ▫ *Jatri* (Traveller : letters from abroad)
1930	▫ *Sahaj path* - parts I & II (text book) ▫ *Ingreji sahaj siksha* - parts I & II (text book) ▫ *Patha parichay*, parts II-IV (text book)
1931	▫ *Shapmochan* (a muscial drama) ▫ *Russiar chithi* (Letters from Russia) ▫ *Nabin* (a musical piece) ▫ *Banabani* (poems)
1932	▫ *Parisesh* (collection of poems) ▫ *Punascha* (collection of poems) ▫ *Kaler jatra* (two dramatic pieces)
1933	▫ *Chandalika* (The Untouchable Woman : a drama) ▫ *Tasher Desh* (Kingdom of Cards : a musical drama) ▫ *Bansari* (The Flute : a drama)
1934	▫ *Malancha* (a novel) ▫ *Char Adhyay* (Four Chapters : a novel) ▫ *Sraban gatha* (collection of songs)
1935	▫ *Bithika* (Avenue : collection of poems) ▫ *Sesh saptak* (collection of poems)
1936	▫ *Shyamali* (poems) ▫ *Patraput* (poems) ▫ *Chhanda* (essays on Bengali prosody)
1937	▫ *Biswaparichay* (article on modern physical astronomy) ▫ *Khapchhara* (rhymes) ▫ *Kalantar* (essays)

	□ *Shay* (children's stories)
	□ *Chharar chhobi* (rhymes)
1938	□ *Senjuti* (poems)
	□ *Bangla Bhasha Parichay* (a treatise on the Bengali language)
	□ *Prantik* (poems)
1939	□ *Shyama* (a dance drama)
	□ *Prahasini* (The Smiling One : poems)
	□ *Akash pradip* (poems)
1940	□ *Nabajatak* (The newly born : poems)
	□ *Sanai* (The Pipe : poems)
	□ *Rog sajyay* (In the sick-bed : poems)
	□ *Tin songi* (Three companions : short stories)
	□ *Chhelebela* (My boyhood days : reminiscences)
1941	□ *Sabhyatar sankat* (Crisis in civilization : an essay)
	□ *Janmadine* (Birthday : poems)
	□ *Arogya* (Recovery : poems)
	□ *Galpo salpa* (stories and verses for children)

Works in English

1912	□ *Gitanjali (Song Offerings)*: a collection of 103 poems translated by author from his poetical works in Bengali viz., *Gitanjali* (51), *Gitimalya* (17), *Naivedya* (16), *Kheya* (11), *Sishu* (3), *Chaitali* (1), *Smaran*(1), *Kalpana* (1), *Utsarga* (1), *Achalayatana* (1).
1913	□ The Gardener : collection of poems translated by author from his poetical works in Bengali - *Kshanika, Kalpana, Sonar Tari, Chaitali, Utsarga, Chitra, Manasi, Mayar Khela, Kheya, Kari O Kamal, Gitali and Saradotsav*
	□ The Crescent Moon : child poems. Most of the poems are from *Sishu.*
	□ Chitra : a drama (translation of Chitrangada)
	□ Sadhana : The Realisation of Life (essays).
	□ One hundred poems of Kabir - translated by Tagore

1916	□ Fruit Gathering : poems translated by author from *Gitali, Gitimalya, Balaka, Utsarga, Katha, Kheya, Smarana, Chitra* etc.
	□ Hungry Stones and other stories: 12 stories.

1. The Hungry Stones (*khudita pashan*)
2. Victory (*jay parajoy*)
3. Once there was a King (*asambhava katha*)
4. Lord, the Baby (*khokababur pratyabartan*)
5. The Kingdom of cards (*tasher desh*)
6. Devotee (*boshtomi*)
7. Vision (*dristidaan*)
8. Babus of Nayanjore (*thakurda*)
9. Living or dead (*jibito o mrito*)
10. We crown thee King (*rajtika*)
11. Renunciation (*tyaga*)
12. Kabuliwala.

6. An examination of the above list will clarify that the major writings of Rabindranath Tagore, especially poetry, were published until early 1920s. His writings after 1920s were not popular as those which were published before 1920. Of course, many of his later writings published after 1920 were excellent from socio-philosophical point of view but could not attract the common Bengalee readers.

7. It is also notable that Rabindranath Tagore wrote several plays after 1920. Many learned critics have undervalued the quality and standard of his plays. Even the famous South Indian playwright Girish Karnad recently said late in 2012 that Rabindranath Tagore was a great poet but a second rate playwright. The following noted news quotes (dated November 09, 2012 and on other dates), will help the readers to better understand it. Girish Karnad stirred up a controversy by launching an attack on Nobel laureate Rabindranath Tagore. Mr. Karnad called Tagore a 'great poet but a second rate playwright.' According to Mr. Karnad, Rabindranath Tagore's greatness as a poet is there, his greatness as a thinker is there but he wrote plays, he certainly was a pioneer in breaking away from the unexciting commercial plays. He did not direct great plays. The point is that he was a mediocre playwright, according to Mr. Karnad.

(*See*:
http://www.hindustantimes.com/News-Feed/Chunk-HT-UI-HomePage-Books/
Girish-Karnad-now-calls-Rabindranath-Tagore-second-rate-playwright/Article1-
957323.aspx)

8. As far as the circumstances which led to Rabindranath getting the Nobel Prize, we are pleased to refer herein below from an article published by Mr. Subrata Kumar Das in *The Daily Star,* Dhaka on 8th May, 2013. He said that Rabindranath, not at all well-known outside India before the publication of his *Gitanjali* (*Song Offerings*) in its English version in November 1912 from London, made millions of people sit up and take notice of him through the prize. It is interesting that Rabindranath never proposed a name for the Nobel from India or from any other country, though he obtained the right to nominate after winning the prize in 1913. It is a well-known fact that among the eighteen members of the Nobel Literature Committee, only the orientalist Esaias Henrik Vilhelm Tegner (1843-1928) knew some basic Bengali. Excepting him, *Gitanjali* (*Song Offerings*) could make no impression on the other members. Moreover, as far as we know most of the Committee members did not read or see the book. The book *Gitanjali (Song Offerings)* has been appended in full in the Appendix of this book for the evaluation of the esteemed readers of this book. Noted individuals and organizations propose nominations to the Nobel Committee. Recommending the name of Rabindranath Tagore, one was a Fellow of the Royal Society of Literature in England. No other nomination came for Rabindranath Tagore. In 1913, the Society proposed the name of the noted British poet and fiction writer Thomas Hardy (1840-1924). As a Fellow and individual member of the society, T. Sturge Moore proposed the name of Rabindranath Tagore in his personal capacity. He wrote to the Secretary of the Nobel Committee of the Swedish Academy in Stockholm as below:

> 'Sir,
> As a Fellow of the Royal Society of the United Kingdom, I have the honour to propose the name of Rabindra Nath Tagore as a person, qualified, in my opinion, to be awarded the Nobel Prize in Literature.
> T. Sturge Moore.'

Moore's letter was the only single document on the basis of which a judgment on Rabindranath could be made. The work before the committee was *Gitanjali* (*Song Offerings*).

10. I have been studying as to the popularity of Rabindranath Tagore's literature from his early days till his passing away and found that his popularity increased geometrically only after his receiving the Nobel Prize for literature in 1913. I wrote about the subject in many places in the Internet and there were many responses from the readers from around the world. Many readers were not satisfied by my short writings and opinions expressed therein due to the absence of references. I reserved the references for my future use. Below I quote one of my Internet submissions:

> I published some observations in several blogs as to the popularity of Rabindranath Tagore. We the Bengalis deeply respect him for his beautiful writings and songs.
>
> A few words about the Nobel Prize for Rabindranath Tagore:
>
> 1. Tagore was presented as an Anglo-Indian before the Nobel Committee. This was never disclosed by Visva Bharati;
>
> 2. Ignoring Americans, it was for the first time that the Nobel Prize for literature was awarded to a non-European;
>
> 3. Interestingly, Tagore never visited the Swedish Academy for about 7 years even after the award (when he was awarded the Nobel Prize he was in England and not in Calcutta);
>
> 4. Tagore never made any contact or speech marking the Nobel Prize (he just made a two-line acknowledgement only);
>
> 5. The British Ambassador (Minister: having the status of *Cherge d'Affaires?*) received Tagore's Nobel Prize in person;
>
> 6. The prize medal was delivered in Calcutta;
>
> 7. None of the Nobel Committee members either knew Bengali well or ever read Tagore's writings; and

8. The library of the Swedish Academy had no book by Tagore accessioned in its record at that time. What do these points signify?

I do not want to interrupt anybody. I understand that Rabindranath Tagore is sacrilege to many of his fans. But the truth should not be suppressed by way of propaganda.

I cordially welcome the objectively substantiated replies to my above points. In fact, if can get such satisfactory replies then I shall surely stop my project on the subject towards publication of a book. Even Swedish Academy confirmed some of the above points.

By my survey results it appears that 80% of popularity of Rabindranath Tagore is due to his getting the Nobel Prize. At least the facts reveal it. I take this opportunity to say that no book on the history of Bengali Literature ever mentioned even the name of Rabindranath Tagore until 1912 when the poet was about 52 years of age.

My above observations are not based on the figments of imagination but available facts.

I am looking forward to objectively substantiated replies with good references, if any.

Replying to my above queries and observations many responses came and some of those were really notable as summarized below:

Referring to Points 1 & 2: It was mentioned by many that the list of nominees for the 1913 Nobel Prize for Literature is now public. *See:*

http://www.nobelprize.org/nobel_prizes/literature/nomination/nomination. php?action=simplesearch&string=1913&start=1. He is referred to in the nomination database as being Indian, not Anglo-Indian: But it must be noted that in 1912-13 everybody understood that the phrase 'Anglo-Indian' meant a British settler in the colonial India. Still it refers to their siblings.

http://www.nobelprize.org/nobel_prizes/literature/nomination/nomination. php?action=show&showid=918. However, in the Award Ceremony speech, the Chairman of the Nobel Committee of the Swedish Academy referred to Tagore as an Anglo-Indian poet with the intention of diverting the attention of the audience, as because this was for the first time that the Nobel Prize for literature was given outside Europe and that also to a native of coloured origin. http://www.nobelprize.org/nobel_prizes/literature/laureates/1913/press.html. Later in the speech, he also referred to Bengal as an Anglo-Indian province. Since India was still part of the British Empire at the time, this was probably the most politically correct reference he could make and also explains why British officials were the intermediaries. The speech, in any case, explains in some detail why Rabindranath Tagore was awarded the Nobel Prize that year (rather than any of the other 31 nominees, who included Thomas Hardy). Referring to Point 3: Tagore received news of the award on 14 November 1913, when he was in Santiniketan (i.e., neither in England, nor in Calcutta), through a telegram from a fellow Bengali poet, Satyendranath Datta. As you may note, the First World War started a few years later and ended in 1918. Indeed, no Nobel Prize for Literature was awarded either in 1914 or in 1918. Referring to Points 4 &5: At the Nobel Banquet on December 10, 1913, the British Chargé d'Affaires read out a telegram from Tagore in accepting the award as follows: "I beg to convey to the Swedish Academy my grateful appreciation of the breadth of understanding which has brought the distant near, and has made a stranger a brother." Referring to Point 6:

According to the 1996 Sahitya Academy book: *A Miscellany – Rabindranath Tagore*, "At a special ceremony in Calcutta on 29 January 1914, Lord Carmichael, Governor of Bengal, delivered the medal and citation to Tagore. For details *see* Prasanta Kumar Pal, *Rabi Jibani*, Vol. VI, Calcutta 1993, p. 455. Referring to Points 7 & 8: The process for selecting the winner of the Nobel Prize for Literature takes over a year. But in the case of Rabindranath Tagore it was surprisingly considered virtually in a few weeks. This will become clear when in the later part of this book I quote a message from Carola Hermelin of Swedish Academy (*see* Chapter 11, Paragraph: 10). http://www.nobelprize.org/nobel_prizes/literature/nomination/. The Nobel Prize was awarded on the basis of Tagore's own English translations of his Bengali poems (particularly *Gitanjali: (Song Offerings)* (1912) in English, which had been published by the India Society of London in November 1912), after being nominated privately by Thomas Sturge S. Moore, a Fellow of the Royal Society of Literature. As mentioned in the award speech: "Tagore's *Gitanjali: (Song Offerings)* (1912), a collection of religious poems, was the one of his works that especially arrested the attention of the selecting critics. Since last year the book, in a real and full sense, has belonged to English literature, for the author himself, who by education and practice is a poet in his native Indian tongue, has bestowed upon the poems a new dress, alike perfect in form and personally original in inspiration. This has made them accessible to all in England, America, and the entire Western world for whom noble literature is of interest, quite independently of any knowledge of his Bengali poetry, irrespective, too, of differences of religious faiths, literary schools, or party aims, Tagore has been hailed from various quarters as a new and admirable master of that poetic art which has been a never-failing concomitant of the expansion of British civilization ever since the days of Queen Elizabeth." Such observation is just mere defensive. The Nobel Prize certainly opened doors for Tagore and led to invitations from all over the world. It led to his being regarded primarily as a poet and a philosopher – something of a mystic. Bengalees, though, are more aware of other aspects of his legacy, such as his songs, his paintings, his educational philosophy, his environmental awareness, and the innovative, semi-classical dance style he created. Travels made Tagore more aware of different cultures and underlined in his mind the need to find ways to allow his Bengali writing to cross linguistic and cultural barriers. They clearly had an influence on Tagore's own body of work, and particularly his use of dance and the dance style itself. This latter development was the subject of the doctoral research by Kaberi Chatterjee – *see* her blog at: http://www.kaberi.eu. It is quite normal for high profile awards to bring international attention to recipients whose work has not previously been recognized widely. In the film world, winning an Oscar has provided a turning point in the careers of many actors. Today many non-Bengalees, even in India, are unaware of Tagore's work, in spite of its timeless, universal qualities and in spite of the Nobel Prize the critics of my above queries opined. Some articles during his 150th birth anniversary have drawn attention to this. See, for example:

http://www.guardian.co.uk/commentisfree/2012/apr/29/rabindranath-tagore-poet-india and http://www.guardian.co.uk/commentisfree/2011/may/07/rabindranath-tagore-why-was-he-neglected.

11. However, it must be stated here that Rabindranath Tagore is the most remarkable literary genius of the Bengali literature, even at present, especially due to the official over-care of Calcutta, Dhaka and Delhi. But the popularity of Tagore among the common readers continues to be on decline.

12. It is notable that after the passing away of the great poet Rabindranath Tagore his prominence was revived by the film maker Satyajit Ray for some years.

13. This has been nicely stated by Andrew Robinson in his book entitled: *Satyajit Ray: The Inner Eye*, published by Andre Deutsch Limited in 1989 from London. It will be relevant to refer to Andrew Robinson' book (pages: 46-47). According to Andrew Robinson (Rabindranath) Tagore and (Satyajit) Ray are 'dissolubly' bound. If non-Bengalees know Tagore at all today, it is mainly by virtue of Ray's interpretations of him on film. Of course, in Bombay, Bimal Roy's film based on Rabindranath's works gave him an all-India popularity, especially by *Do Bigha Zamin*.

14. Satyajit Ray passed away several years back. But the revival of Rabindranath's literature could not be possible without his support. Rabindranath's literatures declined with lesser number of readerships; his getting Nobel Prize for literature a century ago has been gradually entering into the black-hole of the literary universe, if the common readers of the Bengali language, both in the Bengali language and in translation, are concerned. However, about 200 beautiful songs (out of more than 2,000) are still remembered by the Bengalees (particularly in West Bengal of India and in Bangladesh) alone even in the second decade of the 21ˢᵗ century.

———

Chapter 2

British occupation of India and patronage to non- Muslims

1. During the Middle Ages the Christian states of Europe failed to become completely successful in defeating the Muslim countries and lost finally in regaining Constantinople which is known today as Istanbul of Turkey.

2. However, the British Navy was most powerful in the world in those days. The Britishers turned to the Muslim ruled India.

3. Most of the states of India, until the early 16th century, were under the rule of Mughal Emperors. The Mughals were powerful and they were ruling strongly. For the local purpose the Mughals were strong enough to command and control virtually the greater part of the Indian sub-continent. But it may be noted that the Mughals did not have any substantial naval power to face the challenge of the British Navy, co-shared by the East-India Company. The East-India Company was raised under the Royal Charter in London. Hence, the East-India Company always got the maximum support from the then British Navy and subsequently the support and patronage of London.

4. Every critic of history must acknowledge the tactful and far-sighted calculations of London to launch a programmed British Raj in India by defeating the Muslim rulers with the sympathy and support of the non-Muslims of the region.

5. The East-India Company was doing good commercial activities and by applying their tactful diplomacy secured permission from the then Mughal rulers for using the ports in Bombay and Madras. Subsequently they looked into the Bengal region. With the help of high officials of the East-India Company they purchased three villages named Calcutta (corrupt form of Kalighat), Govindapur and Sutanuti. These three villages together comprised of the present-day city of Calcutta. As per historical reports the East-India Company's official Job Charnok purchased the said three villages now known as the city of Calcutta, from the year 1680 to 1689 with the approval of the Mughal Emperor in Delhi.

6. After the purchase of the three villages now consisting of the city of Calcutta, the East-India Company started their expansionist activities. They took up their project of making Calcutta as their seat of ruling India. Here along with their armed forces they established one Fort, naming it as Fort William. The Fort William continued expanding.

7. It is reported that a big portion of land was purchased from the big land owners, among whom one was Dwarkanath Tagore, the grandfather of Rabindranath Tagore. The old Fort William was shifted to this newly purchased big land by the side of the river Ganges (locally known as the Bhagirathi river), which is known as the Fort William today.

8. After becoming well organized and established, the East-India company, considering the psychology of the majority people of the 17th century Bengal, became more enthusiastic and active.

9. During their early occupation of Calcutta the East-India Company made good study of the local population of Bengal, Bihar (including the present day Indian province Jharkhand) and Orissa. The Britishers organized their forces and also imported many learned people from abroad with a view to expanding Christianity in the area. In fact, conversions of mostly the Hindus into Christianity was a success story under the British Raj in India. Today there are millions of the native Christians converted from the Hindus and they are mostly attached to the Roman Catholic Church or the Anglican Church of England.

10. The Britishers established the British Raj in India by occupying the Muslim empires. As such, the Britishers could easily feel that the defeated Muslims were their main antagonists in the then Indian sub-continent. So they planned and programmed all their administrative and political activities accordingly.

11. The Britishers found that the big traders and businessmen in Bengal were Hindus, mostly non-Bengalees. They obtained good commercial response from them and subsequently these non-Bengalee businessmen also extended all support both by men and money to get prepared to fight against the Muslim rulers in the area of greater Bengal, consisting of Bengal, Bihar (including the present day Indian province Jharkhand) and Orissa.

12. With the support of the local Hindu businessmen and the betraying Army Chief of the Nawab, Mir Jafar, the Britishers were successful in defeating and killing the Muslim ruler of the greater Bengal Nawab Sirajud Daulah in the battle of Palassy in 1757. Thus the Britishers became the ruler of greater Bengal. So began the first British colony in the Indian sub-continent and thus began the British rule (The British Raj) in the eastern part of India.

13. By defeating the regional ruler Nawab Sirajud Daulah in 1757, the East-India Company became the virtual ruler of the greater Bengal. They collected and paid various taxes in part to the Mughal emperor of Delhi annually for several years. Later on we find that they expanded the British Raj by defeating various states, mainly those of the Muslim in India.

14. The Britishers invaded various Muslim States in India. But unlike Europe and the Middle-East, no other Muslim countries came forward for the protection of the Muslim Empires of India against the British attacks. This so happened apparently because the Arabs, the Turks and other Muslim countries never treated the Muslims of India as their religious compatriots, rather as natural-born Indian emperors and rulers. From the history we find that there were several appeals to the Middle-Eastern rulers with no response. Thus the Britishers successfully expanded their colonies in India with the help and cooperation from amongst the Hindus who welcomed the British rule against the Muslim rulers. The Britishers chose the Hindus, particularly the Brahmins and the affluent Hindus. The Britishers trained the Hindus with higher education and absorbed them in various spheres of administration.

During the first one hundred years of the British Raj no Indian Muslim was appointed in the higher administrative service.

15. In the next Chapters we may see more details about the absorption of the Hindus to further strengthen the British administration of the then India under the British Raj.

———————

Chapter 3

Rabindranath Tagore followed the foot-steps of *Raja* Ram Mohan Roy and such others

1. In early years the Britishers chose the rich Hindu businessmen, with emphasis to the Brahmins, as their associates in local administration. There were two sectors of the British interests: A. commercial and financial interests and B. administrative and colonial interests. As far as the commercial interests are concerned the Britishers received all cooperation from the non-Bengalee Hindu businessmen. With their support the Britishers were successful in defeating Nawab Sirajud Daulah in the Battle of Palassy in Murshidabad in 1757. Thereafter, the Britishers concentrated their administration of Bengal with the help of superior class of the educated Bengalee Hindus. In the earlier days of the British Raj they received maximum cooperation from the personalities like *Prince* Dwarkanath Tagore, *Raja* Ram Mohan Roy and Ishwar Chandra *Vidyasagar* and like many others. With the help of these people the British rulers made various social reforms to improve the social conditions of the Bengalee Hindus. Importantly they abolished the *Sutee* system of cremating the widow of deceased Hindu husband and also made many other social reformations.

2. Next, they also introduced the law of Permanent Settlement of land with the help of Sun-Set law, which abolished the land rights of almost all the major Muslim-owned properties in Bengal by putting into auction of the Muslim properties which were mostly purchased by the then affluent Hindu businessmen.

3. With various reformations the superior class of the Hindus became the native associates of the Britishers both in administration and in commerce. *Raja* Ram Mohan Roy, the founder of the Brahmo Samaj, a reformed sect of the Hindus abandoning idolatry under the influence of Christianity as propagated by the Britishers, kept a very close contact with the Britishers, who helped him to visit England where he died. He was buried in Bristol.

4. Likewise Ishwar Chandra *Vidyasagar* was appointed the Principal of Sanskrit College of Calcutta. The Britishers also established Hindu College (now Presidency College). It may be noted that at the same time Calcutta Madrassah was founded for the studies of Arabic, Persian and Islamic theology, but never a Muslim was allowed to become its Principal until the last day of the British Raj in India in 1947.

5. In addition, the Britishers expanded the academic programmes of the Fort William College creating wide opportunity of learning Indian culture, tradition and languages. Widely famous Christian priest William Carey helped establishing Bengali and English printing press and published many books in English as well as in Bengali language under his patronage. Thus the Britishers brought in the promotion of the printing and publishing the Bengali, English land other language books. I remember to have seen the Baptist Mission Press in Calcutta engaged in printing of various Christian literatures in about 140 languages. Interestingly it also published a translation of the Holy Quran in Bengali with pro-Christian interpretations.

6. During these days *Shri* Ramkrishna also developed a new Hindu spiritual theory and he was followed by his successful disciple *Swami* Vivekananda who was also helped in visiting various parts of India and subsequently various parts of Europe and America. He became famous globally after his famous speech in a world religious conference held in Chicago. Born in 1861, Rabindranath Tagore also followed the footsteps of *Raja* Ram Mohan Roy and *Swami* Vivekananda who became acquainted with Europe and America.

7. Rabindranath Tagore was the key administrator of the vast property inherited from his grandfather *Prince* Dwarakanath Tagore, who was perhaps the richest Bengalee in the then Bengal.

8. Rabindranath Tagore's father Debendranath Tagore was a very orthodox minded person and he mostly kept himself engaged in the propagation of Brahmo Samaj philosophy. After his father's demise Rabindranath Tagore became the Secretary of Brahmo Samaj. Like his forefathers Rabindranath Tagore and all his family members were supporters of the British Raj until his death in 1941. It is notable that he never gave his full hearted support to *Mahatma* Gandhi's *Swaraj Movement* towards Self-Rule of India.

9. Rabindranath Tagore was so much a supporter of the Britishers that he often used to visit Whiteways & Ludlow's, an exclusive mega shop for the Britishers and other Europeans on House No. 7 of Chowringee Road of Calcutta nearby the big Muslim locality of central Calcutta. But we do not find any record that he ever visited these Muslim localities until his death in 1941. One of the famous Bengalee poets Kazi Nazrul Islam used to live in this locality during the life-time of Rabindranath Tagore. Nor we find any record that shows that Rabindranath Tagore ever visited any Muslim's residence during his life-time. But it is reported that he personally patronized the Hindu-owned shopping mall named Kamalalaya at Dharamtalla Street in central Calcutta.

10. The residence of the Tagore family was located at Jorasanko area, within a mile from the Calcutta University and College Street area. Most of the famous Bengalee Hindu writers and intellectuals of the time lived within two square miles of the Calcutta University and, as such, Rabindranath had the opportunity of close contacts regularly with those writers and intellectuals until the end of his life.

————————

Chapter 4

The influence of *Prince* Dwarakanath Tagore

1. We have noted that after the British Raj began in the United Bengal following the fall of *Nawab* Sirajud Daulah in 1757, and the majority non-Muslims welcomed the Britishers as the antagonists of the Muslim rule in Bengal.

2. When Rabindranath attained mature age he found that the Britishers must be welcomed as the replacement of the Muslim rule. He very cordially welcomed the British Raj. In his famous song: *Janagana Mana Adhinayaka Jayahey...* (which is the national anthem of India today), he welcomed the British Raj as the "Captain" of the will of the people of India. Obviously by the people of India he meant the non-Muslim indigenous peoples of India! This explicitly suggests that he treated the Muslims who lived and ruled India for about 7 (seven) centuries, as the "outsiders"—though they had been living and ruling the major areas of the entire Indian sub-continent as sons of the soil within the meaning of *Bhumiputra*. It is also notable that Muslims adopted the local Hindi language naturally using many common Arabic and Persian words, giving it the form in Persian script called today "Urdu". As we stated earlier the grandfather of Rabindranath, Dwarkanath Tagore established huge land properties in the United Bengal measuring hundreds of acres of land and built dozens of buildings by becoming a very trusted friend of the British Raj. Rabindranath Tagore became a keen follower of his grandfather. In fact, the Britishers most cordially welcomed the sincere and continued support and loyalty of all the Tagore family members.

3. It is true that the Britishers ruled in greater Bengal (including Bihar, Jharkhand and Orissa) very ruthlessly. Of course, they extended all patronage to the superior Bengalee Hindus in every sphere of administration and education. The Muslims of the then Bengal were never given such opportunities. The Bengalee Hindus never looked at this undemocratic and despotic attitude of the Britishers, obviously because the British Raj was most welcome to them against the native Muslim Rule.

4. Rabindranath along with *Raja* Ram Mohan Roy, Ishwar Chandra *Vidyasagar*, Michael Madhusudan Datta and Bankim Chandra Chatterjee and other non-Muslim intellectuals received exclusive patronage from the Britishers.

5. In the central India, it is said, the Britishers were successful in propagating secretly through a section of Muslim *Mullahs* that they should not learn English as it was the language of the Christians. For nearly two centuries the Muslims did not learn English. Also it is notable that in the then Bengal, the frustrated Muslims did not widely learn even the Bengali language, because in those days the Bengali language at the academic levels was much under the impact and influence of the dead Sanskrit language and Hindu scriptures.

6. The Bengalee Hindus never encouraged for the education of the Bengalee Muslims. This distance continues even in the 21st Century.

7. As far as the population of Calcutta during the 19th century is concerned, it grew fast. Massive requirements for the construction of roads, building structures and related works, many Biharies and others from North and Central India came to Calcutta, making it the most populated city of India. Among these working classes of people there were many Urdu-speaking Muslims and most of them became permanently settled in various areas of Calcutta.

8. Even today those areas are called the Muslim areas, namely Colutola, Narkeldanga, Taltalla, Phulbagan, Park Circus, Tatibagan, Tollyganj, Matiaburj, Alipore and Khidderpore etc.

9. Many of the above Muslim immigrants were settled in Calcutta and married many Bengali-speaking Muslims. As a result, the Urdu language of Calcutta Muslims became slightly mixed-up with the Bengali language, at least outside

their residence in the city life. The syntax and pronunciation of Calcutta Urdu became influenced by the local Bengali language.

10. Rabindranath, though known as a Brahmo, he was a deep and devout follower of puritan Hinduism. His literatures amply reflect this.

11. As the Tagore family of Jorasanko of Calcutta was most reliable and trusted Bengalee Hindu family of the British rulers, they always patronized them. Before 1920s we never find Rabindranath-protesting the British Raj in India even for the political consumption of the alert non-Muslims of India.

12. The writings of Rabindranath Tagore being awarded the Nobel Prize for literature in 1913 were very natural reflections of the published literatures in Sanskrit. In fact, *Gitanjali* (*'Song offerings'* – meaning as such in Sanskrit), which was chiefly named for the Nobel Prize, was a collection of poems selected from several of his book of poems. I have dealt with this in more details in the next and the following Chapters.

———————

Chapter 5

The influence of Kalidas, Lalon Fakir and D. L. Roy etc.

1. Rabindranath Tagore was awarded the Nobel Prize for literature in 1913. After the award of Nobel Prize Rabindranath Tagore started becoming popular in Bengal and also in the Western countries. More details about this growing popularity shall be discussed in the later part of this book.

2. In writing his poems and songs Rabindranath was very much influenced by Kalidas, Lalon Fakir and also by D. L Roy. He was also influenced by several other spiritual writers both of the East and of the West. It may be pointed out here that he was very much influenced by Lalon Fakir whose songs were very popular in Bengal by the end of the nineteenth century. Some critics also believe that Rabindranath borrowed from many songs of Lalon Fakir. It is obvious that many of his songs were influenced by the songs of Lalon Fakir.

3. None can deny the fact that Rabindranath Tagore was a writer of extraordinary genius and talent. He applied his genius to his songs and music with those of Bengal keeping the spiritual value of Hindu religious songs, especially the melody of Folk songs by adding the tone and temper of the Western music.

4. It is true that he followed Lalon Fakir, Atul Prasad Sen and D.L Roy. But it is notable that he never adopted Islamic music and Ghazal pattern as was done by Kazi Nazrul Islam, a noted popular Bengalee Muslim poet of the 20th century.

5. As such, Rabindranath's writings were growing more popular among the Bengalee Hindus. Surprisingly, the Bengalee Muslims could not much appreciate the literature ascribed to Rabindranath Tagore. But it seems that lately some Bengalee Muslim readers and writers in Bangladesh have emerged as appreciators of Tagore's writings.

6. Rabindranath's songs and writings were gaining popularity, though in slower speed, in the first and second decades of the 20th century. But after his getting the Nobel Prize he became more and more popular among the Bengalee Hindu readers.

7. It is true that Rabindranath's songs are of high value and appeal. He composed more than two thousand songs and poems. But is also notable that only about two hundred songs remain popular and have remained classic among the Bengalees. This is also true even after his one hundred fiftieth year of birth anniversary. However, generally no appreciator of Rabindranath's songs can name more than two hundred songs of the poet today.

8. In spite of many attempts Tagore songs could not gain any popularity among the Indians outside of Bengal.

9. As the mystical Baul Songs (which style is the chief rhythm of the songs of Lalon Fakir and the same of Rabindranath Tagore) are not well known to many, particularly outside South Asia (especially India and Bangladesh). According to various scholars the Bauls of Bengal belong to a heterodox devotional *(bhakti)* tradition which was influenced by all three major religions of the Indian subcontinent-Hinduism, Buddhism, and Islam - and yet is distinctly different from each of them. They *come* primarily from economically and socially marginal groups, and live on the fringes of both Hindu and Muslim society. [*See*: Donald S. Lopez (ed). Princeton University Press, 1995), pp. 187-208]

———————

Chapter 6

'Terrorist movement' in Bengal

1. It is true, as we have noted earlier, that the Britishers were all along patronizing the Bengalee Hindus in all walks of life, but their ruthless colonialism, hatred towards the coloured Indian peoples and disrespect to the religious values of the Indians - of Hindus, Muslims, Buddhists and Jains as well created a continued opposition in the region.

2. Not to speak of the Muslims from whom the Britishers snatched their kingdoms by force and conspiracy, even many Hindus started realizing the continued bitter effect of the colonial British Raj in India. This became slowly wide and wider. The British rulers could smell that the educated Indians have started feeling the bad aspects of the expanding British colonialism in India. With a view to suppressing such feelings for freedom the Britishers patronized the making and shaping of All India National Congress under the leadership of a Bengalee W. C. Banerjee in 1885, which ironically led to the 'Quit India' movement under the leadership of *Mahatma* M. K. Gandhi. However, it is also notable that various anti-British movements by the common people were growing slowly but intensively in the Eastern India, from Patna to Dhanbad; Calcutta to Darjeeling; Shillong to Dhaka and Chittagong. These movements were branded by the Britishers as the "Terrorist Movement". The British rulers strongly resisted the actions taken by the Indian patriots during the last part of the 19th century and the first part of 20th century.

3. When we read history, even those by the Western writers, we all can realize the ruthlessness of the colonial rulers in the British-Indian sub-continent. The hanging of a minor school boy Khudiram Bose became one of the saddest parts of the history of Bengal. The Bengalee people, regardless of religion and sex were deeply disturbed by the cruel British rulers. This was even felt by the British administration both in Calcutta and in London.

4. Tactfully Britishers tried to appease the Bengalees, especially the Bengalee Hindus by giving them high positions in the administration as doctors, engineers, professors and in the Civil Services. It is in this process they picked-up up the name of Rabindranath Tagore, belonging to the pro-British Tagore family of Jorasanko, Calcutta, which was all time loyal to the British colonial rulers in India.

5. Many members of the Brahmo Samaj were opposed to the British Raj. But all the members of Tagore family remained very faithful to the British Raj and its continuity.

6. The Britishers were pampering the trusted Tagore families of Jorasanko of Calcutta. But simultaneously for their colonial gains, obviously, they were thinking of change in their relationship with the Indians in general which led to the shifting of the capital of British India from Calcutta to Delhi in 1911. The plan of Lord Curzon in partitioning of the united Bengal was purely a British scheme of dividing the Bengalee Muslims and the Bengalee Hindus. Also we shall see later in this book how the Britishers enforced the partition of India in 1947 with the help of Lord Mountbatten, obtaining full consent from Sardar Ballabhbhai Patel, *Pundit* Jawaharlal Nehru, and *Mahatma* M. K. Gandhi.

———————

Chapter 7

British colonial rulers' continued patronage of the elite non-Muslims

1. Since the first partition of Bengal in 1905 the Bengalees of all communities lived together peacefully is spite of the fact that the British rulers kept the Muslims, who became majority religious population under the British rule in Bengal, fully deprived of notable appointments in the administration. There was hardly one or two Muslim doctors and engineers and professors etc. in any district of Bengal. More notably the higher education as well as the learning of the English language was not extended to the Bengalee Muslims. They were deprived of getting appointments to any high public Civil Service.

2. The greatest of all damages the Britishers caused to the Bengali Muslims was the Permanent Settlement law by which the Britishers sold away in auction more than 80 percent of the land properties held by the Muslims in Bengal (including both West Bengal of India today and the territory of Bangladesh) and this process also gave *Prince* Dwarkanath Tagore to acquire huge properties both in West Bengal of India and in the territory of Bangladesh of the 21st century.

3. From the early British occupation of Bengal in 1757, the Britishers occupied various other Muslim States in the Central and the Northern areas of India. With the occupation of further Muslim States in India the Britishers caused banishment of many Muslim States' high influential persons or officials to

specific areas of Calcutta like Matiaburj, Alipore, Ripon Street, Marsden Street of Taltala and Park Circus etc. We know among these people were the children and family members of Tipu Sultan of Mysore who was killed by the Britishers. Even the Britishers started doubting many other important Muslim leaders and intellectuals, like the famous Urdu poet Mirza Ghalib, who was interned in Calcutta for two years.

4. Also Wazed Ali Shah of Oudh was banished to Calcutta. All historical records of such banishments were destroyed by the Britishers. The emergence of Dwarkanath Tagore as the biggest landlord of Bengal, as stated before, holding hundreds of acres of land in Jorasanko and Pathuria Ghata Street of Calcutta; in present day Esplanade- BBD Bagh near Chowringhee and other areas was also possible due to British patronage. He also acquired perhaps nearly one thousand acres of land in other areas accumulating huge wealth. He perhaps became the richest man of the undivided Bengal under the British Raj.

5. As we have noted earlier that for the development of Calcutta was needed big labour force which attracted thousands of unemployed and poor Muslim families from Bihar, Jharkand, Orissa and other parts of the British occupied Raj in India.

6. A large number of Muslims came to Calcutta and settled permanently in various areas and got married with the local Bengalee Muslims. But it is notable that mostly such mixed Muslim families switched to the Urdu language with local linguistic influence rather than Bengali. In some cases where Bengali was used in home, but Urdu was adopted as the educational language. This can be found in Calcutta even today.

7. The Britishers were very successful in creating socio-cultural and religious differences between the Muslims and the Hindus. The Calcutta Muslim areas were strongly under the vigilance of the British rulers. Perhaps for this reason that more of the converted Christians along with the Jews were living in the areas of central Calcutta. On the eve of the partition of India in 1947, there were three Christian burial grounds and more than twenty-six churches, for the Roman Catholics, Protestants, Anglicans and Baptists in the central Calcutta, mostly from Bow Bazaar to Park Street areas.

8. Subsequently the Britishers established the present day New Market and now defunct shopping mall at house number seven Chowringee Road, Calcutta in the name of Whiteways and Ludlow's. It was a big shopping mall for the Britishers and the rich people of Calcutta. Rabindranath Tagore and his family members regularly used to go to this Shopping mall for the purchase of various luxury items with the opportunity of meeting the Europeans. During the early years of partitioned India the shopping mall was winding up in the year 1949. As a boy of very young age I had the opportunity of visiting this shopping mall. Later on in the same premises the United States Information Service Library was started and operated for many years. Today a part of it in the Western side is running the Big Bazaar, an Indian shopping mall.

———————

Chapter 8

Shifting of capital from Calcutta to New Delhi

1. As we have stated in the last Chapter, the British rulers were deeply concerned with the sporadic terrorist movements in Bengal, Bihar and Orissa. During this period London was seriously thinking of better and more comfortable seat of administration as the capital of India preferring Delhi where they made massive construction of secretariat buildings, parliament building, supreme court building and many other offices.

2. The Britishers, however, continued their policy of patronizing the Bengalee Brahmin Hindus for getting their support and sympathy in administration.

3. It is notable that the majority of the people who took the leadership of the terrorist movements were non-Brahmins and the Britishers took the advantage of their divide and rule policy. Since the time of Lord Curzon the Britishers took the policy of the partition of Bengal and enforced it in the year of 1905 with a view to helping the Bengalee Brahmin Zamindars who became the big land owners of the East Bengal, and made the Bengalee Muslims pleased with the Muslim majority areas in the East Bengal.

4. Today every student of India's history well understands that the Britishers partitioned the united Bengal in 1905 for the better protection of the interests of the Bengalee Hindus who became a religious minority in this province. The

Britishers have always been a covert people. This we find everywhere they had their colonial rule.

5. Of course, many Bengalee Hindus, including Rabindranath Tagore, misunderstood the spirit of the British plan of partition of Bengal in 1905. Many launched movement protesting the partition of the United Bengal in 1905. The Britishers realized that the feelings of the Bengalee Hindu elite class against the partition of Bengal in 1905, and eventually annulled it in 1911.

6. Subsequently, New Delhi became the capital of India with new pomp and grandeur. Also came the support of the non-Bengalee bureaucrats. The Britishers shifted their capital from Calcutta to New Delhi after more than twenty decades since their purchase of the lands consisting of three villages now constituting the city of Calcutta, in 1680-89. But it is notable that they had to quit India before the end of four decades after shifting to New Delhi under the great leadership of *Mahatma* M. K. Gandhi of All India National Congress, which was also founded by the supporters of the British Raj in India.

7. The Britishers who ruled India for about two hundred years were so close to the Hindus that it was quiet possible for Lord Mountbatten to convince *Mahatma* Gandhi to refrain from his demand for the United India in a two hours' secret meeting. This has been stated by the former president of Indian National Congress and who later on became a Minister of divided India in the cabinet of Jawaharlal Nehru as Education Minister. In his book "*India Wins Freedom*" (the "complete version" published in 2011 by Orient Blackswan Private Limited, Asaf Ali Road, New Delhi) *Maulana* Azad explicitly stated so. *Maulana* Azad said that Sardar Patel and even Jawaharlal had become supporters of partition, Gandhiji remained his only hope. During this period Gandhiji was staying at Patna. He had earlier spent some months in Noakhali (now in Bangladesh) where he made a great impression on local Muslims and created a new atmosphere of Hindu-Muslim unity. It was expected that he would come to Delhi to meet Mountbatten and he actually arrived on 31 March. *Maulana* Azad went to see him at once and his very first remark was, "Partition has now become a threat" It seems, Mahatma Gandhi added, Vallavbhai and even Jawaharlal had surrendered. Mahatma Gandhi also said, "What a question to ask! If the Congress wishes to accept partition, it will be over my dead body. So long as I am alive I will never agree to the partition of

India. Nor will I, if I can help it, allow Congress to accept it." Later that same day Gandhiji met Lord Mountbatten. He saw him again the day next and again on 2 April. Sardar Patel came to him soon after he returned from his first meeting with Lord Mountbatten and was closeted with him for over two hours. What happened during this meeting *Maulana* Azad said that he did not know. But when he met Gandhiji again, according to him, he received the greatest shock of his life to find that he had changed. He was still not in favour of partition but he no longer spoke so vehemently against it. What surprised and even shocked *Maulana* Azad more was that Mahatma Gandhi began to repeat the arguments which Sardar Patel had already used in favour of the partition of India. (*See* pages: 202-203 of the above imprinted book entitled: *India Wins Freedom* by *Maulana* Abul Kalam Azad).

8. *Maulana* Abul Kalam Azad was a significantly important Muslim leader of the All India National Congress, who also was President of All India National Congress. But he, being a minority Muslim leader of the All India National Congress was too insignificant in exercising his power and influence in the ultimate political decision of the All India National Congress in 1946 on the partition of India. *Maulana* Abul Kalam Azad later became Education Minister under the Prime Minister Jawaharlal Nehru who also simultaneously appointed *Sardar* Vallabhbhai Patel as his Home Minister.

9. *Mahatma* Gandhi's one undivided India concept failed under the British pressure and similarly it is notable that lord Curzon's partition of Bengal policy of 1905 to divide the Muslims and the Hindus of Bengal was reintroduced in 1946 with the help of Shyama Prasad Mukherjee, the President of Hindu Mahasabha ignoring the proposed United Bengal supported by leading personalities like the Prime Minister of Bengal Shahid Suhrawardy belonging to the All India Muslim League and leading personalities like Sharat Chandra Bose (brother of the great anti-colonial Bengalee leader *Netaji* Subhas Chandra Bose) and Kiran Shankar Roy, both belonging to the All India National Congress.

10. The Britishers partitioned India and went away leaving their invisible spirit of 'divided rule policy' which led to the killing of more than ten million people since 1946 and dividing millions of families of the Indian sub-continent. But the beneficiaries of the partitioned India never looked at this humanitarian

issue even after about seventy years. This is a black chapter in the history of governance of India, Pakistan and Bangladesh. There was never a joint meeting or consultation on the subject comprising of India, Pakistan and Bangladesh. Nor the United Nations ever looked at this sad problems arising out of the killing, looting and burning of millions. The United Nations and the big Western Powers shed much crocodile's tears even with 10% calamities in other parts west of Indian-Subcontinent. Only God knows if any such feelings will ever be coming up in the minds of the political and social leaders of these three artificially partitioned countries by the Britishers.

———————

Chapter 9

Brahmo Samaj & Tagore

1. Brahmo Samaj or Brahmo Dharma was a reformed school of the Hindus under the impact of Islam and Christianity. It is notable here that under the impact and influence of Islam, the Christians became divided into Roman Catholics and Protestants. When the Britishers started ruling Bengal after defeating *Nawab* Sirajud Daulah in 1757, many of the Western Christian Priests started propagating Christianity and converted many Hindus into Christianity, among those most prominent was Michael Madhusudan Datta.

2. The Hindus of today in India are the British founded united front of the idol worshipers and other peoples belonging to the four castes of Bhahmins, Kshatriyas, Vaishyas and Sudras. Sudras of today's Hindu community of India perhaps consists nearly 80 per cent of the Hindu community of India. Sudras do not have equal social and religious rights as those of the Brahmins, Kshtriyas and the Vaishyas. On this point one may point out the voting rights of the Sudras. Yes, they have the voting rights but they are socially programmed only to vote for the Brahmins, Kshtriyas and the Vaishyas. As a result, in India, the world's biggest Democracy only the Brahmins, Kshtriyas and the Vaishyas are elected to the Parliament. Therefore, in India today mostly the 20 percent caste Hindus rule the country along with some Muslims and Christians. This is the inner picture of India's democracy. The Brahmins always despised the Tagore family of Rabindranath Tagore. Most of the Bengalee Hindus are very secular. But outside Bengal the Hindus are more orthodox. This is the reason that Rabindranath was never allowed to enter the Jagannath Temple in Puri of Orissa.

3. I have given the above detailed quotation so as to give the readers a comprehensive idea about the school of Brahmos, which has virtually merged with the mainstream of the conventional Bengalee Hindus of India, and other Hindu fanatic factors of today.

4. Though Rabindranath Tagore is rarely explicit about the influence of Islam and Muslims in his writings and social life, still it is well known that his father learnt Persian very well and appreciated the great Persian writers until his death.

5. Rabindranath Tagore partially inherited the Islamic traditional taste of his father, read and appreciated Persian literature and also travelled through Iran. Like his father he also adopted the long robe like the Iranian Ayatollahs. Even his sister Swarnakumari Devi wrote a novel named *Hooghly Imambari* based on the life of Haji Mohammad Mohsin, a famous pious Muslim.

6. All critics and appreciators of the literatures left by Rabindranath Tagore were under the influence of Christianity, Islam and Judaism.

7. However, it is important to note that the central point of the Rabindranath Tagore literatures grew based on the principles of Hindu philosophy under the impact of *Vadas, Upanishads, Puranas, Ramayana* and *Mahabharata* etc.

8. In addition, towards the end of his life the complexity of his faith became intelligible, as if he became less of a Hindu or Brahmo and more of a Pantheistic Free-Thinker hoping for achieving a global unity in human values and called for a Universal Religion in tune with the modern Western Political Philosophy (*vide* his *The Realization of Life* and other spiritual writings and lectures) under the shadow of subtle pagan belief emphasizing on *Karma* and in the existence of many gods and deities. In general, the faith of Hinduism is based on the principles of Pantheism. It varies from place to place according to local custom and practice even within India today.

———————

Chapter 10

Rabindranath Tagore's Western and Jewish contacts

1. Following the footsteps of *Raja* Ram Mohan Roy and *Swami* Vivekananda, Rabindranath Tagore undertook his multiple travels to the West (both in Europe and in Americas) and he established wide contacts with the eminent Western personalities. The more details are available in various biographies on Rabindranath Tagore.

2. Rabindranath Tagore was so much under the spell of the Westerners that by the age of thirty he had made scores of contacts with Western men and women. He was not academically qualified beyond school, but he made good studies in English and by the age of twenty he read several plays by William Shakespeare and translated his famous drama *Macbeth* into Bengali.

3. Jesus Christ, in whose name Christianity is founded, is the greatest historic name of the prominent Jews. He was born as a Jew, lived long and died as a Jew and was lastly buried perhaps in Kashmir of India. His burial place is shown in Srinagar of Kashmir and the name of the road is Jesus Road. His mother Mary reportedly died in Murree of Pakistan. The name Murree is coined word from Mary and Marium, mother of Jesus.

4. The Jews are followers of Abraham and Moses and are called the "chosen people of God". After the rise of the Roman Empire the Jews, who were mostly

concentrated in Egypt and in the West Asia became widely scattered all over Europe and, particularly after the Second World War, in different parts of the Western world and other places, including India. With the co-operation of the Britishers and the United States emerged the sovereign state of Israel. It was founded after the Second World War, ignoring the rights of the Palestinians, the sons of the soil.

5. The Jews always maintain secrecy as to their religious values, customs and practice and life-styles. Since the last century they have been living in a way mixed-up with that of the Christians. The religion of the Jews is inherited by birth and not by conversion.

6. Many British Jews were associated with the administration of the British Raj in India, but in public they were not identified as Jews. The Jews are expert in high level intelligence and secret service.

7. Rabindranath Tagore's grandfather Dwarakanath Tagore is known to be having very close relationship with the British Raj high officials, many of whom were Jews. In three decades Dwarakanath Tagore became a billionaire and the biggest landlord of Bengal.

8. Rabindranath Tagore had established close contacts with many influential Jews. The most important contact was with William Rothenstein, who was of German origin and a British national. It was he who introduced Rabindranath Tagore with the famous poet W. B. Yeats, who wrote the introduction to the English version *Gitanjali* and Thomas Sturge Moore, who proposed the name of Rabindranath Tagore for the Nobel Prize for literature in 1913. The Nobel Committee, perhaps, better understood the meaning and content of Yeats's introduction to *Gitanjali* than the actual translated poems of the book.

9. Here it will be quite relevant to reproduce below in Kumud Biswas's words from the Internet that for successful lobbying Tagore needed to have published at least one book in a language which was known to the selectors. Rothenstein himself belonged to a German Jewish family. His father had immigrated to Britain only a few years ago in 1859. According to Tagore's biographer Krishna Kripalani, William Rothenstein (1872-1945) was the bridge that helped Tagore to cross over from his little world of Bengal to the big world of the West. We

have seen that their acquaintance was a sheer accident and it took place when Rothenstein visited the house of the Tagores in January, 1911 and saw the poet there for the first time in his life. Before that he did not even hear about him. It is therefore interesting to know how it happened.

[See: http://www.boloji.com/index.cfm?md=Blogs&sd=Blog&BlogID=722#sthash. pOzKNuf6.dpuf]

10. We also know that the English translations of Rabindranath Tagore's writings were compiled and published by E. J. Thompson.

11. Apart from William Rothenstein and E. J. Thompson, Rabindranath Tagore had many Jewish contacts. It is also notable that the founder of Nobel Prize, Alfred Nobel himself was a Jew. Later on, of course, we also know about his close contacts with the well-known Jewish scientist Albert Einstein, with whom Rabindranath Tagore had several well known interviews and correspondences.

12. In 1941 when Rabindranath Tagore passed away the leading Jewish periodical *Jerusalem Post* of Israel published the following news datelined August 08, 1941 headlining that 'Tagore, Friend of Jews and Zionism, Dies in Calcutta'. It was stated that Rabindranath Tagore, India's poet and Nobel Prize winner, and a staunch friend of Jews and Zionism, died on August 08, 1941 at the age of 80 in Calcutta. The story added that Tagore, who had world-wide fame as a poet and philosopher, frequently expressed his opposition to the Nazi atrocities against the Jews. He also expressed "deep sympathy for the aims and aspirations of Zionism." In a statement made recently, it was added that Tagore said: "I regard Jewish nationalism as an effort to preserve and enrich Jewish culture and tradition. I visualize a Palestine Commonwealth in which the Arabs will live their own religious life and the Jews will revive their resplendent future, but both will be united as one political and economic entity."

13. Everybody knows that the Jews had very influential link with the government in London during the past centuries as is today.

14. Rabindranath Tagore openly supported the Jews and Zionists. It was so much so that a road in Israel was named after him as "Rehov Tagore".

[See: http://www.jpost.com/Magazine/Features/Student-Life-Rehov-Tagore-Ramat-Aviv]

15. The above contacts of Rabindranath Tagore remain more or less unknown to the readers even today. As a matter of fact he had many more Jewish contacts both known and unknown. If extended research is done scores of Jewish contacts of Rabindranath Tagore can be found. The Jews and Zionists from different countries kept contacts with him. Impressed by his friendly attitude towards the Jews and Zionists, even the Russian Nobel Laureate and a Jew, Boris Pasternak translated his poem in Russian.

16. However, Rabindranath Tagore's contacts with the Americans and the Britishers are widely known. In fact, Rabindranath Tagore was so much appreciator of the British Raj in India that even today he is respected by the Britishers.

17. The news lately published also imprints the respect of the Britishers towards their friendly and obedient Indian literary genius Rabindranath Tagore. Prince Charles unveiled bust of Rabindranath Tagore in the centre of London in the year 2011 to coincide with the 150th anniversary of Tagore's birth. (See: *The India Post*, New Delhi; dated July 8, 2011)

Chapter 11

The Nobel Prize for Literature in 1913

1. As stated in the above chapters, we have noted that Rabindranath Tagore followed the footsteps are *Raja* Ram Mohan Roy and *Swami* Vivekananda etc. and he undertook extensive foreign visits and lecture programmes in Europe and America.

2. None can deny that he was an extraordinary literary genius. In his various lecture programmes he did impress and influence many in the Western countries by presenting his spiritual philosophy based on *Vedas, Upanishads* and *Puranas,* the ancient Hindu scriptures in Sanskrit and the great ancient Indian philosophical values. Until the end of the 19th century such philosophical values remained unknown to many European and American peoples. As such, Rabindranath Tagore was gaining more popularity in the West with his literary contributions and paid lectures.

3. Rabindranath was a very well known supporter of the British Raj in India as were his ancestors and most of his family members and relations. Considering such attitude of the Tagore family the Britishers all way extended all the best possible patronage to him.

4. Up to the first decade of the 20th Century Rabindranath became acquainted with many eminent Europeans, especially the Britishers.

5. The details are not available but it is fact that the then Crown Prince of Sweden made visits to Calcutta and was acquainted with Rabindranath Tagore before his getting nomination for the Nobel Prize for literature in 1913. There are some romours that Rabindranath was inspired by his Western contacts that an English translation of his poems and its publication in the book-form would be welcome. He himself translated his various poems into English during his leisure time staying in the Eastern part of Bengal by the side of river Padma (now in Bangladesh).

6. Rabindranath's collected English translation of these poems, well known as *Gitanjali* was highly appreciated by his Western acquaintances. W.B. Yeats read his English translation of the Bengali poems which he named *Gitanjali (Song Offerings)*. In 1912 the English version was published by India Society of London with a beautiful introduction by W.B. Yeats. *Gitanjali (Song Offerings)* in English was published in limited circulation of two hundred fifty copies, which was not, perhaps, even sufficient for distribution amongst his friends and acquaintances. This edition of *Gitanjali (Song Offerings)* in English has become so rare today that the original edition of the book is not available even in India, including in the National Library of India in Calcutta.

7. England was interested to see that more honour should be given to Rabindranath Tagore, the most loyal supporter of the British Raj during those days.

8. One Thomas Sturge Moore, a member of the Royal Society of Literature in London, nominated Rabindranath for being considered for the award of the Nobel Prize for Literature in 1913. Thomas Sturge Moore was not a famous personality in England in those days.

9. On July 23, 2010 on the reference of Jonna Patterson of the Nobel Foundation, I wrote an email letter to Carola Hermelin, Assistant to the Secretary of the Nobel Committee of the Swedish Academy. The text of my email letter dated July 23, 2010 is as quoted below:

From: <u>Abul Shamsuddoulah</u>
To: <u>carola.hermelin@svenskaakademien.se</u>
Cc: <u>info@nobel.se</u>
Sent: Friday, July 23, 2010 8:32 AM

Subject: How Rabindranath Tagore was awarded the 1913 Nobel Prize for literature?

Dear Ms. Carols Hermelin:

We are a new book publisher ... in Dhaka, Bangladesh ... In this connection, for one book on Rabindranath Tagore's getting 1913 Nobel Prize, we urgently need some information from your end.

Days ago we wrote to: Ms. Jonna Patterson, Informator / Public Relations Officer, The Nobel Foundation.

She was kind enough to direct us to contact you for the required information as furnished below:

1. Who nominated the name of Rabindranath Tagore for the 1913 Nobel Prize for Literature?

2. Who else were short-listed authors for consideration for the 1913 Nobel Prize for Literature?

3. Before the Swedish Academy / the Nobel Foundation finally decided to give the 1913 Nobel Prize for Literature to Rabindranath Tagore who was being top considered for the 1913 Nobel Prize for Literature?

4. We understand that there were 12 members in the prize giving committee for deciding the 1913 Nobel Prize for Literature. Reportedly, only one member saw / read the English version of Rabindranath Tagore's book of poems *Gitanjali* published from with a total circulation of 250 only. How far these facts are correct?

5. Did Rabindranath Tagore ever made any prize acceptance speech as is customarily done?

6.   Did he receive the prize in person or it was received through somebody else? If the latter happened then who did receive the prize and how it was delivered to Rabindranath Tagore?

7.   Did Rabindranath Tagore ever visited and lectured in the Swedish Academy / the Nobel Foundation after the 1913 Nobel Prize for Literature? <u>We shall be grateful to get any other relevant information on the subject</u>. Your information will be authentic and we shall be pleased to use yours comparing those received from Stockholm in the past.

Please be assured that immediately after the publication of the book it will be air mailed to you, if you so desire.We thank you very much for condidering our request with priority.
Looking forward to hearing from you.
Best regards.
Yours truly,

A. B. M. Shamsud Doulah

10. Replying to my above letter Carola Hermelin of the Swedish Academy replied to me on July 27, 2010 as below:

From: Carola Hermelin carola.hermelin@svenskaakademien.se
To: Abul Shamsuddoulah shamsuddoulah@yahoo.com
Sent: Tuesday, July 27, 2010 21:12:10
Subject: Re: How Rabindranath Tagore was awarded the 1913 Nobel Prize for literature?

Dear Sir / Madame,

First some general background to your questions. The Nobel Committee of the Swedish Academy consists of five members from the academy. These five members are entrusted with the responsibility of preparing the academy's discussion of the award. The academy is not bound to follow the recommendations of the Nobel committee. The decision is taken by all members of the academy. The academy has eighteen members. In order for the voting to get valid it is required that at least twelve members of the academy shall take part and that the candidate shall receive more than half of the votes.

The members of the committee in January 1913 were Harald Hjärne (chairman), Karl Alfred Melin, Erik Axel Karlfeldt, Esaias Tegnér d. y. and Hans Hildebrand. However Hans Hildebrand passed away in February 1913. His place in the committee was taken by Per Hallström.

On 1st February 1913 the Nobel committee made the decision to send to the members of the academy a list of all the candidates and also a typed copy of the nomination ltters of the candidates.

The answers to your questions are as follow:

1. T. Sturge Moore, member of the Royal Society of Literature in London.

    2. On 24th September 1913 the Nobel Committee of the Swedish Academy decided to recommend the Swedish Academy to give the French professor Emile Faguet the prize. Emile Faguet had been nominated by Ém. Boutroux, member of the French Academy.

2. Verner von Heidenstam, a member of the Swedish Academy who was not a member of the Nobel Committee, sent on 18th October 1913 a letter to the permanent secretary of the academy, Erik Axel Karlfeldt. In this letter Heidenstam argues for that the prize should be given to Tagore.

    The academy had a meeting on 23rd of October. In the record for this meeting the academy refers to the letter of Verner von Heidenstam and also to the fact that a new work by Tagore had been published in English translation. The academy recommends the Nobel committee of the Swedish Academy to reconsider Tagore for the prize.

    The Nobel committee followed the recommendation of the academy. The Nobel committee decided on their meeting on 30th October to send to all members of the academy two statements by Per Hallström concerning Tagore.

    On the 13th November the final decision was taken by the academy to give Tagore the prize. The minutes of the academy are confidential so there is no possibility to say exactly how many members of the academy voted for Tagore. However there must have been a majority who voted for Tagore (See above).

The new English translation referred to by the academy on the meeting on the 23rd of October could be either The Garderner (1913) or Glimpses of Bengal life (1913) or both. These translations are in the Nobel Library of the Swedish Academy.

The members of the academy had also read Gitanjali (1913) in English translation. The Nobel Library ot the Swedish Academy had at least two copies of that book who circulated among the members of the academy. There was also one member of the Nobel Committee who could read Bengali; Esaias Tegnér d. y. He borrowed from the Nobel Library of the Swedish Academy three works; Naivedya, Kheya and Gitanjali in Bengali.

6. He did not receive the prize in person in Stockholm. It was received by M. Clive, the English Minister.

7. In 1921 Tagore visited Stockholm. He then met some of the members of the Swedish Academy; Per Hallström, Erik Karlfeldt, Hjalmar Hammarskjöld, Anders Österling and Sven Hedin at a dinner. He was also in Stockholm in September 1926 invited by Sven Hedin.

Yours sincerely,

Carola Hermelin
Assistant to the Secretary of the Nobel Committee of the Swedish Academy

11. Both the above quoted two email messages are very important for the better understanding of how Rabindranath Tagore was awarded the 1913 Nobel Prize for literature?

12. As far as I know the 1912 original edition of *Gitanjali* (Song Offerings), published in London in English was not recorded in the Accession Register of the Swedish Academy Library in 1912 before receiving the nomination for Rabindranath Tagore, a writer of different region and language. In addition, it is a logical absurdity that there could be other publications of Rabindranath Tagore in the Swedish Academy's library before such nomination. As a writer Rabindranath Tagore was almost an unknown person to Europe before 1912. Nobody expects the presence of a book of poems in Korean or Bulgarian or Greek language in any library in Bangladesh, India or Pakistan. Yes, it is very likely that multiple copies of 1912 edition of *Gitanjal (Song Offerings)* were

furnished to the Swedish Academy library after or with the Rabindranath Tagore's nomination.

13. Further it is notable that in September 1913 the Nobel Committee of the Swedish Academy decided to recommend the Swedish Academy to give the Nobel Prize to French Professor Emile Faguet. Emile Faguet had been nominated by a member of the French Academy. Later on, as we see above, a member of the Swedish Academy who was not a member of the Nobel Committee, in a letter dated October 18, 1913 addressed to the Permanent Secretary stating that the prize would be given to Rabindranath Tagore though he was not in the short-list of the candidates recommended for the Nobel Prize in 1913. This process of consideration of the recommended authors is notable.

14. The appreciation of W.B. Yeats and W.H. Auden came up but they never reported to have recommended Rabindranath Tagore for the Nobel Prize.

15. In addition there is no evidence that any member of Nobel Committee knew Bengali well to understand *Gitanjali (Song Offerings)* poems in original Bengali. It is true that the Crown Prince of Sweden visited Calcutta a few years before 1913 not because he knew Bengali but because of the fact that in those days Calcutta was a big cultural city and the Capital of the British Raj.

16. Of course, also it is not known if Rabindranath Tagore had any acquaintance with the Nobel Prize Committee members.

———————

Chapter 12

Rabindranath Tagore was awarded Nobel Prize as an 'Anglo-Indian' poet

1. As stated above Rabindranath was not in contact or had any communication with any of the Nobel Committee members before the announcement of the Nobel Prize in 1913.

2. It is also apparent that the Nobel Committee members did not know that Rabindranath Tagore was a native Bengalee. It becomes clear from the speech of the Chairman of the Nobel Committee. It is notable that *Harald Hjärne, Chairman of the then Nobel Committee of the* **Swedish Academy** called him an "Anglo Indian Poet" during the prize giving ceremony. It will be relevant here to quote his full speech which is now widely available in the Internet. We all know that by the phrase "Anglo-Indian" in 1913 everybody understood the person to be a Britisher settled in India. Thousands of Britishers were settled as such and there exists three burial grounds commemorating such "Anglo-Indians". However, the said speech is quoted below from:

http://hindufocus.wordpress.com/2010/05/09/why-was-tagore-given-the-nobel-prize/ Home.

The above is quoted as such because the 'Hindu Focus' importantly highlights (shown in bold prints) some portions of the speech with questions and comments, which are given after the complete quotation:

The Nobel Prize in Literature 1913: Presentation Speech

Presentation Speech by Harald Hjärne, Chairman of the Nobel Committee of the Swedish Academy, on December 10, 1913

In awarding the Nobel Prize in Literature to the **Anglo-Indian poet, Rabindranath Tagore**, the Academy has found itself in the happy position of being able to accord this recognition to an author who, in conformity with the express wording of Alfred Nobel's last will and testament, had during the current year, written the finest poems «of an idealistic tendency.» Moreover, after exhaustive and conscientious deliberation, having concluded that these poems of his most nearly approach the prescribed standard, the Academy thought that there was no reason to hesitate because the poet's name was still comparatively unknown in Europe, due to the distant location of his home. There was even less reason since the founder of the Prize laid it down in set terms as his «express wish and desire that, in the awarding of the Prize, no consideration should be paid to the nationality to which any proposed candidate might belong.»

Tagore's *Gitanjali: Song Offerings* (1912), a collection of religious poems, was the one of his works that especially arrested the attention of the selecting critics. Since last year the book, in a real and full sense, has belonged to English literature, for the author himself, who by education and practice is a poet in his native Indian tongue, has bestowed upon the poems a new dress, alike perfect in form and personally original in inspiration. This has made them accessible to all in England, America, and the entire Western world for whom noble literature is of interest and moment. Quite independently of any knowledge of his Bengali poetry, irrespective, too, of differences of religious faiths, literary schools, or party aims, **Tagore has been hailed from various quarters as a new and admirable master of that poetic art which has been a never-failing concomitant of the expansion of British civilization** ever since the days of Queen Elizabeth.

The features of this poetry that won immediate and enthusiastic admiration are the perfection with which the poet's own ideas and those he has borrowed have been harmonized into a complete whole; his rhythmically balanced style, that, to quote an English critic's opinion, «combines at once the feminine grace of poetry with the virile power of prose»; his austere, by some termed classic, taste in the choice of words and his use of the other elements of expression in a borrowed tongue – those features, in short, that stamp an original work as such, but which at the same time render more difficult its reproduction in another language.

The same estimate is true of the second cycle of poems that came before us, *The Gardener, Lyrics of Love and Life* (1913). In this work, however, as the author himself points out, he has recast rather than interpreted his earlier inspirations. Here we see another phase of his personality, now subject to the alternately blissful and torturing experiences of youthful love, now prey to the feelings of longing and joy that the vicissitudes of life give rise to, the whole interspersed nevertheless with glimpses of a higher world.

English translations of Tagore's prose stories have been published under the title *Glimpses of Bengal Life* (1913). Though the form of these tales does not bear his own stamp – the rendering being by another hand – their content gives evidence of his versatility and wide range of observation, of his heartfelt sympathy with the fates and experiences of differing types of men, and of his talent for plot construction and development.

Tagore has since published both a collection of poems, poetic pictures of childhood and home life, symbolically entitled *The Crescent Moon* (1913), and a number of lectures given before American and English university audiences, which in book form he calls *Sâdhanâ: The Realisation of Life* (1913). They embody his views of the ways in which man can arrive at a faith in the light of which it may be possible to live. This very seeking of his to discover the true relation between faith and thought makes Tagore stand out as a poet of rich endowment, characterized by his great profundity of thought, but most of all by his warmth of feeling and by the moving power of his figurative language. Seldom indeed in the realm of imaginative literature are attained so great a range and diversity of note and of colour, capable of expressing with equal harmony and grace the emotions of every mood from the longing of the soul after eternity to the joyous merriment prompted by the innocent child at play.

Concerning our understanding of this poetry, by no means exotic but truly universally human in character, the future will probably add to what we know now. We do know, however, that the poet's motivation extends to the effort of reconciling two spheres of civilization widely separated, which above all is the characteristic mark of our present epoch and constitutes its most important task and problem. **The true inwardness of this work is most clearly and purely revealed in the efforts exerted in the Christian mission-field throughout the world**. In times to come, historical inquirers will know better how to appraise its importance and influence, even in what is at present hidden from our gaze and where no or only grudging recognition is accorded. They will undoubtedly form a higher estimate of it than the one now deemed fitting in many quarters. Thanks to this movement, fresh, bubbling springs of living water have been tapped, from which poetry in particular may draw inspiration, even though those springs are perhaps intermingled with alien streams, and whether or not they be traced to their right source or their origin be attributed to the depths of the dreamworld. More especially, **the preaching of the Christian religion has provided in many places the first definite impulse toward a revival and regeneration of the vernacular language, i.e., its liberation from the bondage of an artificial tradition, and consequently also toward a development of its capacity for nurturing and sustaining a vein of living and natural poetry.**

The Christian mission has exercised its influence as a rejuvenating force in India, too, where in conjunction with religious revivals many of the vernaculars were early put to literary use, thereby acquiring status and stability. However, with only too regular frequency, they fossilized again under pressure from the new tradition that gradually established itself. But the influence of the Christian mission has extended far beyond the range of the actually registered proselytizing work. The struggle that the last century witnessed between the living vernaculars and the sacred language of ancient times for control over the new literatures springing into life would have had a very different course and outcome, had not the former found able support in the fostering care bestowed upon them by the self-sacrificing missionaries.

It was in Bengal, the oldest Anglo-Indian province and the scene many years before of the indefatigable labours of that missionary pioneer, Carey, to promote the Christian religion and to improve the vernacular language, that Rabindranath Tagore was born in 1861. He was a scion of a respected family that had already given evidence of intellectual ability in many areas. The surroundings in which the boy and young man grew up were in no sense primitive or calculated to hem in his conceptions of the world and of life. On the contrary, in his home there prevailed, along with a highly cultivated appreciation of art, a profound reverence for the inquiring spirit and wisdom of the forefathers of the race, whose texts were used for family devotional worship.

Around him, too, there was then coming into being a new literary spirit that consciously sought to reach forth to the people and to make itself acquainted with their life needs. This new spirit gained in force as reforms ere firmly effected by the Government, after the quelling of the widespread, confused Indian Mutiny.

Rabindranath's father was one of the leading and most zealous members of a religious community to which his son still belongs. That body, known by the name of «Brahmo Samaj», did not arise as a sect of the ancient Hindu type, with the purpose of spreading the worship of some particular godhead as superior to all others. Rather, it was founded in the early part of the nineteenth century by an enlightened and influential man who had been much impressed by the doctrines of Christianity, which he had studied also in England. He endeavoured to give to the native Hindu traditions, handed down from the past, an interpretation in agreement with what he conceived to be the spirit and import of the Christian faith. Doctrinal controversy has since been rife regarding the interpretation of truth that he and his successors were thus led to give, whereby the community has been subdivided into a number of independent sects. The character, too, of the community, appealing essentially to highly trained intellectual minds, has from its inception always precluded any large growth of the numbers of its avowed adherents. Nevertheless, the indirect influence exercised by the body, even upon the development of popular education and literature, is held to be very considerable indeed. Among those community members who have grown up in recent years, Rabindranath Tagore has laboured to a pre-eminent degree. To them he has stood as a revered master and prophet. That intimate interplay of teacher and pupil so earnestly sought after has attained a deep, hearty, and simple manifestation, both in religious life and in literary training.

To carry out his life's work Tagore equipped himself with a many-sided culture, European as well as Indian, extended and matured by travels abroad and by advanced study in London. In his youth he travelled widely in his own land, accompanying his father as far as the Himalayas. He was still quite young when he began to write in Bengali, and he has tried his hand in prose and poetry, lyrics and dramas. In addition to his descriptions of the life of he common people of his own country, he has dealt in separate works with questions in literary criticism, philosophy, and sociology. At one period, some time ago, there occurred a break in the busy round of his activities, for he then felt obliged, in accord with immemorial practice among his race, to pursue for a time a contemplative hermit life in a boat floating on the waters of a tributary of the sacred Ganges River. After he returned to ordinary life, his reputation among his own people as a man of refined wisdom and chastened piety grew greater from day to day. The open-air school which he established in western Bengal, beneath the sheltering branches of the mango tree, has brought up numbers of youths who as devoted disciples have spread his teaching throughout the land. To this place he has now retired, after spending nearly a year as an honoured guest in the literary circles of England and America and attending the Religious History Congress held in Paris last summer (1913).

Wherever Tagore has encountered minds open to receive his high teaching, the reception accorded him has been that suited to a bearer of good tidings which are delivered, in language intelligible to all, from that treasure house of the East whose existence had long been conjectured. His own attitude, moreover, is that he is but the intermediary, giving freely of that to which by birth he has access. He is not at all anxious to shine before men as a genius or as an inventor of some new thing. In contrast to the cult of work, which is the product of life in the fenced-in cities of the Western world, with its fostering of a restless, contentious spirit; in contrast to its struggle to conquer nature for the love of gain and profit, «as if we are living», Tagore says, «in a hostile world where we have to wrest everything we want from an unwilling and alien arrangement of things» (*Sâdhanâ*, p. 5); in contrast to all that enervating hurry and scurry, he places before us the culture that in the vast, peaceful, and enshrining forests of India attains its perfection, a culture that seeks primarily the quiet peace of the soul in ever-increasing harmony with the life of nature herself It is a poetical, not a historical, picture that Tagore here reveals to us to confirm his promise that a peace awaits us, too. By virtue of the right associated with the gift of prophecy, he freely depicts the scenes that have loomed before his creative vision at a period contemporary with the beginning of time.

He is, however, as far removed as anyone in our midst from all that we are accustomed to hear dispensed and purveyed in the market places as Oriental philosophy, from painful dreams about the transmigration of souls and the impersonal *karma*, from the pantheistic, and in reality abstract, belief that is usually regarded as peculiarly characteristic of the higher civilization in India. Tagore himself is not even prepared to admit that a belief of that description can claim any authority from the profoundest utterances of the wise men of the past. He peruses his Vedic hymns, his *Upanishads*, and indeed the theses of Buddha himself, in such a manner that he discovers in them, what is for him an irrefutable

truth. If he seeks the divinity in nature, he finds there a living personality with the features of omnipotence, the all-embracing lord of nature, whose preternatural spiritual power nevertheless likewise reveals its presence in all temporal life, small as well as great, but especially in the soul of man predestined for eternity. Praise, prayer, and fervent devotion pervade the song offerings that he lays at the feet of this nameless divinity of his. Ascetic and even ethic austerity would appear to be alien to his type of divinity worship, which may be characterized as a species of aesthetic theism. Piety of that description is in full concord with the whole of his poetry, and it has bestowed peace upon him. He proclaims the coming of that peace for weary and careworn souls even within the bounds of Christendom.

This is mysticism, if we like to call it so, but not a mysticism that, relinquishing personality, seeks to become absorbed in an All that approaches a Nothingness, but one that, with all the talents and faculties of the soul trained to their highest pitch, eagerly sets forth to meet the living Father of the whole creation. This more strenuous type of mysticism was not wholly unknown even in India before the days of Tagore, hardly indeed among the ascetics and philosophers of ancient times but rather in the many forms of *bhakti*, a piety whose very essence is the profound love of and reliance upon God. **Ever since the Middle Ages, influenced in some measure by the Christian and other foreign religions,** *bhakti* **has sought the ideals of its faith in the different phases of Hinduism, varied in character but each to all intents monotheistic in conception. All those higher forms of faith have disappeared or have been depraved past recognition, choked by the superabundant growth of that mixture of cults that has attracted to its banner all those Indian peoples who lacked an adequate power of resistance to its blandishments**. Even though Tagore may have borrowed one or another note from the orchestral symphonies of his native predecessors, yet he treads upon firmer ground in this age that draws the peoples of the earth closer together along paths of peace, and of strife too, to joint and collective responsibilities, and that spends its own energies in dispatching greetings and good wishes far over land and sea. Tagore, though, in thought-impelling pictures, has shown us how all things temporal are swallowed up in the eternal:

Time is endless in thy hands, my lord.
There is none to count thy minutes.
Days and nights pass and ages bloom and fade like flowers. Thou knowest how to wait.

Thy centuries follow each other perfecting a small wild flower.

We have no time to lose, and having no time, we must scramble for our chances. We are too poor to be late.

And thus it is that time goes try, while I give it to every querulous man who claims it, and thine altar is empty of all offerings to the last.

At the end of the day I hasten in fear lest thy gate be shut; but if I find that yet there is time.

(Gitanjali, 82.)

4. Commenting on the *Presentation Speech by Harald Hjärne, the then Chairman of the then Nobel Committee of the* **Swedish Academy, on December 10, 1913, the** *'Hindu Focus'* **(see: Internet) stated that** l*abeling Tagore as an Anglo-Indian poet, in this presentation speech, spills out that the Nobel Prize was not given to him just for his literary excellence. The award came because he was perceived to be a poet who was far removed from traditional oriental philosophy, was a member of the Brahmo Samaj (enlightened, because it was not a sect of ancient Hindu type!), who could be considered as a product of the world-wide rejuvenating force of the Christian mission and a master of the poetic art that was a never-failing concomitant of the expansion of the British civilization. It also added that with such colonial zealots even the Bhakti movement was claimed to be influenced and 'refined' by Christianity!*

5. *In fact, not to speak of identifying Rabindranath Tagore as a Bengalee, he was not even identified as a native Indian.*

6. *However, with a view to avoiding any misunderstanding in the minds of the readers I take the opportunity to quote the above speech again from the official Website of the Nobel Committee below:*

Official Award Ceremony Speech

Presentation Speech by Harald Hjärne, Chairman of the Nobel Committee of the <u>*Swedish Academy*</u>*, on December 10, 1913:*

In awarding the Nobel Prize in Literature to the Anglo-Indian poet, Rabindranath Tagore, the Academy has found itself in the happy position of being able to accord this recognition to an author who, in conformity with the express wording of Alfred Nobel's last will and testament, had during the current year, written the finest poems «of an idealistic tendency.» Moreover, after exhaustive and conscientious deliberation, having concluded that these poems of his most nearly approach the prescribed standard, the Academy thought that there was no reason to hesitate because the poet's name was still comparatively unknown in Europe, due to the distant location of his home. There was even less reason since the founder of the Prize laid it down in set terms as his «express wish and desire that, in the awarding of the Prize, no consideration should be paid to the nationality to which any proposed candidate might belong.»

Tagore's *Gitanjali: Song Offerings* (1912), a collection of religious poems, was the one of his works that especially arrested the attention of the selecting critics. Since last year the book, in a real and full sense, has belonged to English literature, for the author himself, who by education and practice is a poet in his native Indian tongue, has bestowed upon the poems a new dress, alike perfect in form and personally original in inspiration. This has made them accessible to all in England, America, and the entire Western world for whom noble literature is of interest and moment. Quite independently of any knowledge of his Bengali poetry, irrespective, too, of differences of religious faiths, literary schools, or party aims, Tagore has been hailed from various quarters as a new and admirable master of that poetic art which has been a never-failing concomitant of the expansion of British civilization ever since the days of Queen Elizabeth. The features of this poetry that won immediate and enthusiastic admiration are the perfection with which the poet›s own ideas and those he has borrowed have been harmonized into a complete whole; his rhythmically balanced style, that, to quote an English critic›s opinion, «combines at once the feminine grace of poetry with the virile power of prose»; his austere, by some termed classic, taste in the choice of words and his use of the other elements of expression in a borrowed tongue - those features, in short, that stamp an original work as such, but which at the same time render more difficult its reproduction in another language.

The same estimate is true of the second cycle of poems that came before us, *The Gardener, Lyrics of Love and Life* (1913). In this work, however, as the author himself points out, he has recast rather than interpreted his earlier inspirations. Here we see another phase of his personality, now subject to the alternately blissful and torturing experiences of youthful love, now prey to the feelings of longing and joy that the vicissitudes of life give rise to, the whole interspersed nevertheless with glimpses of a higher world.

English translations of Tagore's prose stories have been published under the title *Glimpses of Bengal Life* (1913). Though the form of these tales does not bear his own stamp - the rendering being by another hand - their content gives evidence of his versatility and wide range of observation, of his heartfelt sympathy with the fates and experiences of differing types of men, and of his talent for plot construction and development.

Tagore has since published both a collection of poems, poetic pictures of childhood and home life, symbolically entitled *The Crescent Moon* (1913), and a number of lectures given before American and English university audiences, which in book form he calls *Sâdhanâ: The Realisation of Life* (1913). They embody his views of the ways in which man can arrive at a faith in the light of which it may be possible to live. This very seeking of his to discover the true relation between faith and thought makes Tagore stand out as a poet of rich endowment, characterized by his great profundity of thought, but most of all by his warmth of feeling and by the moving power of his figurative language. Seldom indeed in the realm of imaginative literature are attained so great a range and diversity of note and of colour, capable of expressing with equal harmony and grace the emotions of every mood from the longing of the soul after eternity to the joyous merriment prompted by the innocent Child at play.

Concerning our understanding of this poetry, by no means exotic but truly universally human in character, the future will probably add to what we know now. We do know, however, that the poet's motivation extends to the effort of reconciling two spheres of civilization widely separated, which above all is the characteristic mark of our present epoch and constitutes its most important task and problem. The true inwardness of this work is most clearly and purely revealed in the efforts exerted in the Christian mission-field throughout the world. In times to come, historical inquirers will know better how to appraise its importance and influence, even in what is at present hidden from our gaze and where no or only grudging recognition is accorded. They will undoubtedly form a higher estimate of it than the one now deemed fitting in many quarters. Thanks to this movement, fresh, bubbling springs of living water have been tapped, from which poetry in particular may draw inspiration, even though those springs are perhaps intermingled with alien streams, and whether or not they be traced to their right source or their origin be attributed to the depths of the dreamworld. More especially, the preaching of the Christian religion has provided in many places the first definite impulse toward a revival and regeneration of the vernacular language, i.e., its liberation from the bondage of an artificial tradition, and consequently also toward a development of its capacity for nurturing and sustaining a vein of living and natural poetry.

The Christian mission has exercised its influence as a rejuvenating force in India, too, where in conjunction with religious revivals many of the vernaculars were early put to literary use, thereby acquiring status and stability. However, with only too regular frequency, they fossilized again under pressure from the new tradition that gradually established itself. But the influence of the Christian mission has extended far beyond the range of the actually registered proselytizing work. The struggle that the last century witnessed between the living vernaculars and the sacred language of ancient times for control over the new literatures springing into life would have had a very different course and outcome, had not the former found able support in the fostering care bestowed upon them by the self-sacrificing missionaries.

It was in Bengal, the oldest Anglo-Indian province and the scene many years before of the indefatigable labours of that missionary pioneer, Carey, to promote the Christian religion and to improve the vernacular language, that Rabindranath Tagore was born in 1861. He was a scion of a respected family that had already given evidence of intellectual ability in many areas. The surroundings in which the boy and young man grew up were in no sense primitive or calculated to hem in his conceptions of the world and of life. On the contrary, in his home there prevailed, along with a highly cultivated appreciation of art, a profound reverence for the inquiring spirit and wisdom of the forefathers of the race, whose texts were used for family devotional worship. Around him, too, there was then coming into being a new literary spirit that consciously sought to reach forth to the people and to make itself acquainted with their life needs. This new spirit gained in force as reforms ere firmly effected by the Government, after the quelling of the widespread, confused Indian Mutiny.

Rabindranath's father was one of the leading and most zealous members of a religious community to which his son still belongs. That body, known by the name of «Brahmo Samaj», did not arise as a sect of the ancient Hindu type, with the purpose of spreading the worship of some particular godhead as superior to all others. Rather, it was founded in the early part of the nineteenth century by an enlightened and influential man who had been much impressed by the doctrines of Christianity, which he had studied also in England. He endeavoured to give to the native Hindu traditions, handed down from the past, an interpretation in agreement with what he conceived to be the spirit and import of the Christian faith. Doctrinal controversy has since been rife regarding the interpretation of truth that he and his successors were thus led to give, whereby the community has been subdivided into a number of independent sects. The character, too, of the community, appealing essentially to highly trained intellectual minds, has from its inception always precluded any large growth of the numbers of its avowed adherents. Nevertheless, the indirect influence exercised by the body, even upon the development of popular education and literature, is held to be very considerable indeed. Among those community members who have grown up in recent years, Rabindranath Tagore has laboured to a pre-eminent degree. To them he has stood as a revered master and prophet. That intimate interplay of teacher and pupil so earnestly sought after has attained a deep, hearty, and simple manifestation, both in religious life and in literary training.

To carry out his life's work Tagore equipped himself with a many-sided culture, European as well as Indian, extended and matured by travels abroad and by advanced study in London. In his youth he travelled widely in his own land, accompanying his father as far as the Himalayas. He was still quite young when he began to write in Bengali, and he has tried his hand in prose and poetry, lyrics and dramas. In addition to his descriptions of the life of he common people of his own country, he has dealt in separate works with questions in literary criticism, philosophy, and sociology. At one period, some time ago, there occurred a break in the busy round of his activities, for he then felt obliged, in accord with immemorial practice among his race, to pursue for a time a contemplative hermit life in a boat floating on the waters of a tributary of the sacred Ganges River. After he returned to ordinary life, his reputation among his own people as a man of refined wisdom and chastened piety grew greater from day to day. The open-air school which he established in western Bengal, beneath the sheltering branches of the mango tree, has brought up numbers of youths who as devoted disciples have spread his teaching throughout the land. To this place he has now retired, after spending nearly a year as an honoured guest in the literary circles of England and America and attending the Religious History Congress held in Paris last summer (1913).

Wherever Tagore has encountered minds open to receive his high teaching, the reception accorded him has been that suited to a bearer of good tidings which are delivered, in language intelligible to all, from that treasure house of the East whose existence had long been conjectured. His own attitude, moreover, is that he is but the intermediary, giving freely of that to which by birth he has access. He is not at all anxious to shine before men as a genius or as an inventor of some new thing. In contrast to the cult of work, which is the product of life in the fenced-in cities of the Western world, with its fostering of a restless, contentious spirit; in contrast to its struggle to conquer nature for the love of gain and profit, «as if we are living», Tagore says, «in a hostile world where we have to wrest everything we want from an unwilling and alien arrangement of things» (*Sâdhanâ*, p. 5); in contrast to all that enervating hurry and scurry, he places before us the culture that in the vast, peaceful, and enshrining forests of India attains its perfection, a culture that seeks primarily the quiet peace of the soul in ever-increasing harmony with the life of nature herself It is a poetical, not a historical, picture that Tagore here reveals to us to confirm his promise that a peace awaits us, too. By virtue of the right associated with the gift of prophecy, he freely depicts the scenes that have loomed before his creative vision at a period contemporary with the beginning of time.

He is, however, as far removed as anyone in our midst from all that we are accustomed to hear dispensed and purveyed in the market places as Oriental philosophy, from painful dreams about the transmigration of souls and the impersonal *karma*, from the pantheistic, and in reality abstract, belief that is usually regarded as peculiarly characteristic of the higher civilization in India. Tagore himself is not even prepared to admit that a belief of that description can claim any authority from the profoundest utterances of the wise men of the past. He peruses his Vedic hymns, his *Upanishads*, and indeed the theses of Buddha himself, in such a manner that he discovers in them, what is for him an irrefutable truth. If he seeks the divinity in nature, he finds there a living personality with the features of omnipotence, the all-embracing lord of nature, whose preternatural spiritual power nevertheless likewise reveals its presence in all temporal life, small as well as great, but especially in the soul of man predestined for eternity. Praise, prayer, and fervent devotion pervade the song offerings that he lays at the feet of this nameless divinity of his. Ascetic and even ethic austerity would appear to be alien to his type of divinity worship, which may be characterized as a species of aesthetic theism. Piety of that description is in full concord with the whole of his poetry, and it has bestowed peace upon him. He proclaims the coming of that peace for weary and careworn souls even within the bounds of Christendom.

This is mysticism, if we like to call it so, but not a mysticism that, relinquishing personality, seeks to become absorbed in an All that approaches a Nothingness, but one that, with all the talents and faculties of the soul trained to their highest pitch, eagerly sets forth to meet the living Father of the whole creation. This more strenuous type of mysticism was not wholly unknown even in India before the days of Tagore, hardly indeed among the ascetics and philosophers of ancient times but rather in the many forms of *bhakti*, a piety whose very essence is the profound love of and reliance upon God. Ever since the Middle Ages, influenced in some measure by the Christian and other foreign religions, *bhakti* has sought the ideals of its faith in the different phases of Hinduism, varied in character but each to all intents monotheistic in conception. All those higher forms of faith have disappeared or have been depraved past recognition, choked by the superabundant growth of that mixture of cults that has attracted to its banner all those Indian peoples who lacked an adequate power of resistance to its blandishments. Even though Tagore may have borrowed one or another note from the orchestral symphonies of his native predecessors, yet he treads upon firmer ground in this age that draws the peoples of the earth closer together along paths of peace, and of strife too, to joint and collective responsibilities, and that spends its own energies in dispatching greetings and good wishes far over land and sea. Tagore, though, in thought-impelling pictures, has shown us how all things temporal are swallowed up in the eternal:

Time is endless in thy hands, my lord.
There is none to count thy minutes.
Days and nights pass and ages bloom and fade like flowers. Thou knowest how to wait.
Thy centuries follow each other perfecting a small wild flower.
We have no time to lose, and having no time, we must scramble for our chances. We are too poor to be late.
And thus it is that time goes try, while I give it to every querulous man who claims it, and thine altar is empty of all offerings to the last.
At the end of the day I hasten in fear lest thy gate be shut; but if I find that yet there is time.
(Gitanjali, 82.)
(See http://www.nobelprize.org/nobel_prizes/literature/laureates/1913/press. html)

7. We have already noted that not to speak of identifying the poet as a Bengalee, in fact, he was not even identified as a native Indian.

8. As a matter of fact we see in the speech of Harald Hjarne, Chairman of the then Nobel Committee that he highly appreciated the literary excellence of Rabindranath Tagore; but the main emphasis in his speech was on the secular approach of Rabindranath Tagore's literary values which heralded new possibilities of strong Christian-Hindu relationship and which could strengthen the bond of the British Raj of the Christian West and the Hindu Indians in the East. Everybody knows that Rabindranath was not present during the prize distribution ceremony of the Nobel Prize for Literature in 1913.

9. It is surprising that the speech of the Chairman Harald remains unpublished in India until recent time. Even Vishva Bharati, a publishing house founded and patronized by Rabindranath Tagore himself, in Calcutta never published it. Now from the later part of the 20th century the above quoted speech of Chairman Harold is available in the Internet.

10. From the foregoing chapters it becomes clear that London lobbied for the passage of Nobel Prize award to Rabindranath Tagore. Of course, none can deny the fact that Rabindranath Tagore's literature was of high quality and perhaps is one of the best even if evaluated by the measure of international comparative literature.

———————

Chapter 13

Why Rabindranath Tagore was not present for receiving the Nobel Prize?

1. The first English version of *Gitanjali (Song Offerings)* was published in London by India Association with a circulation of 250 (two hundred fifty) copies only. Obviously most of the copies of the book were distributed among the friends and acquaintances of Rabindranath. As we have noted that not a single copy of the 1912 edition of the book is available with anybody in India today. This fact suggests that it was published but most surely it was distributed or sold outside India. At least the book was less known. The peoples of the European countries were less acquainted with the English language and literature before the First World War which started in 1914. Also we have noted from the historical records that Rabindranath's contacts with the West were mostly either with the British or with the Americans. Therefore, the book was obviously recommended by the *tatbirkars* or the lobbyists for Rabindranath Tagore to the Nobel Committee.

2. According to information available it is clear that Rabindranath had prior knowledge of his nomination for the Nobel Prize. It is not exactly known if he was in Calcutta or in London during that time.

3. We do not find any reason why he did not go to Sweden for receiving the Nobel Prize. Subsequently it was learnt that British diplomat Mr. Clive received the prize for and on behalf of Rabindranath in Stockholm, and later

on the British Governor in Calcutta handed over the prize, which included a medal, a certificate and U.S. Dollars equivalent to several million in current value. In 1921 Rabindranath Tagore visited Stockholm and some members of the Swedish Academy met him. It is also clear from the message from Carola Hermelin, Assistant to the Secretary of the Nobel Committee of the Swedish Academy that the Nobel Prize to Rabindranath Tagore was not given on the recommendation of the Nobel Committee but at the singular instance of the Swedish Academy, which is not the custom and practice in the history of the Nobel Prize.

4. In those days the award of Nobel Prize was so important and famous that he visited Stockholm in 1926. But he did not go to Stockholm in 1913 for receiving the Nobel Prize, perhaps because he was introduced as an "Anglo Indian Poet". The question comes whether it was for hiding his actual identity that he was a native Bengalee. Everybody knows that so far until 1913 the Nobel Prize for literature was never given to any non-European and not even to any American. This impliedly suggests that London obviously promoted Rabindranath Tagore for the prize with its good contacts with Stockholm.

5. There is no evidence or record that Rabindranath Tagore was sick or physically unable to receive the 1913 Nobel Prize. At that time he was about fifty- two years of age.

6. Being a successor to one of the richest families of Bengal, founded by his grandfather Dwarkanath Tagore, Rabindranath Tagore was certainly not in short of fund for his passage to Sweden in 1913. Moreover, in 1912 when he was being considered for the Nobel Prize, various information sources suggest that he was in London. It is also well known that by that time Rabindranath Tagore made several visits to Europe and America.

7. As stated before, by the year 1912 he was almost unknown as a famous writer. In fact, he was not popular even in Bengal. This becomes clearly evidenced from the fact that his name was not even mentioned in the famous fifteen-hundred-page book entitled: *The History of Bengali Language and Literature*, by Dinesh Chandra Sen which was published by the Calcutta University in the year 1912 in English. In 1912 Rabindranath Tagore was 52-years old and had written and published more than three dozens of books of poems, plays

and prose writings. But hardly there were any notable readers' appreciation. Therefore, the question of Rabindranath's popularity in the first decade of the 20th century to the Nobel Committee or for that matter to the European readers does not arise. This is a significantly important point to be noted.

8. For the reasons unknown Rabindranath Tagore neither went to receive the Nobel Prize, nor sent any written speech as is customary with the Nobel Prize recipients. He simply sent a two-line formal telegram acknowledging the acceptance of the prize.

9. It was obvious that being a non-European he was awarded the prize at the instance of London. From the history it is well known that the British rulers in India was having a political and mental gymnastic with the terrorist movement in Bengal during the last decade of 19th century and in the first decade of 20th century. The prize was received not by any of the friends of the poet rather it was received by a British diplomat for and on his behalf. Even in Calcutta the much well-known and the most famous prize was handed over to Rabindranath Tagore in person but not in any official prize presentation ceremony.

10. Only after receiving the Nobel Prize his popularity rose up in a geometrical rate. Naturally he himself became very much inspired by the prize and subsequently produced more and more quality literary publications during the next one decade, as we can find from the chronological list of his publications, fully detailed in the introductory chapter of this book.

11. True, Rabindranath Tagore was a great writer from India and he was a befitting author to be awarded Nobel Prize for literature, but not in accordance with the principles and practice of literary evaluation of the West and the same of the then Nobel Committee. In this connection it may be noted that even the powerful and more widely popular English writer Thomas Hardy was not awarded the prize.

12. But again it may be noted that the writings of Rabindranath were published under the influence of the ancient Indian Hindu literary works, namely the literatures of Kalidas and under the influence of *Vedas, Upanishads, Puranas, Ramayana* and *Mahabharata* which he adopted in the light of Western

literature, for which reason he earned appreciations from the famous Western authors and personalities like W. B. Yeats and W.H. Auden, etc. who later on branded his writings as same old repeated "rubbish". It is so remarked because same or similar types of monotonous writings, with no new massages, were coming from his subsequent literary products especially after 1920.

13. Even recently, as stated earlier, a widely known Indian dramatist Mr. Girish Karnad similarly criticized the standard and quality of the dramas and plays by Rabindranath Tagore. as we can see from the recently published reports on the views of Mr. Karnad (See: September 06, 2014 in Mail Online India; http://www.dailymail.co.uk/indiahome/indianews/article-2230652/ Girish-Karnad-trains-guns-Nobel-Laureate.html)

14. Similarly we also find the immediate reaction in the Western press as to the quality and standard of Rabindranath's poetry. Many such reports were published in the Western press after the announcement of Nobel Prize for Rabindranath in 1913. A report was published in *New York Times*, immediately after the publication of news about the award of the Nobel Prize for literature in 1913, suggesting the impact of the Western literatures. It said that East is East, of course, and West is West, and never the twain shall meet, and the rest of it. But spite of Kipling and his gods, there is more of the East in the West and the West in the East than either is often given credit for. The strength of the fascination which the philosophies of Asia have for Europe can be no better shown than by the frequency with which it is traded upon, and the number of cults whose adherents dream that by some short cut t hey can reach the psychic plane of the Indian mystic. The prevalence of this foolish superstition has brought Orientalism in general into disrepute with certain hardheaded individuals, who would be greatly surprised if they realized how much of the simon-pure article lies in the coaled in their own souls. It is to these, as well as to the initiate, that the poems of Rabindranath Tagore will appeal. As William Butler Yeats says of them, "the work of a supreme culture, they yet appear as much the growth of the common soil as the grass and the rushes." Since the 1913 award of the Nobel Prize to the Indian poet, the details of his life have become so well known that it is not necessary to refer to them here. He is said to be so popular in his own land that people flock to see him pass, and wherever Bengali is spoken his songs are sung by high and low-for like the old minstrels

of the West, he sets his words to music of his own composition. The root of this adoration, for it is little less, is to be found in the words of one of his own countrymen quoted by Mr. Yeats: "All the aspirations of mankind are in his hymns. He is the first among our saints who has not re fused to live, but has spoken out of life itself" the report added.

The work of Rabindranath falls naturally into three divisions: the first, that of early youth, deals largely with nature; the second, to which *The Gardener* belongs, includes love songs and the "intimations of immortality" that accompany, or ought to accompany, happy love; the third is the period of the poet's full maturity, after he has experienced human bliss and sorrow, and has turned to the deep things of the spirit for consolation and reward. Adding further the *New York Times* said in the report that the present translation in a balanced, half-rhythmical prose, is made by the author from the rhymed version of the original. It is naturally impossible for most of us to judge what the lyrics may be like in the Bengali, and we have to take on faith the assertion that they are full of wonderful and unforgettable music and color. It is not difficult to believe it, for Rabindranath Tagore's prose is of singular beauty, strong and delicate, and carved to the minute perfection of an ivory relief. Many of our own poets have sung the passion and the pain of finite yearning after the distant and infinite, but none more simply yet imaginatively than the Indian:

> I am restless. I am athirst for far away things.
> My soul goes out in a longing to touch the skirt of the dim distance.
> O Great beyond. O the Keen call of the flute.
> I forget, I ever forget that I have no wings to fly, that I am bound in this spot evermore.
> I am listless, I am a wanderer in my heart.
> In the sunny haze of the languid hours, what vast vision of thine takes shape in the blue of the sky!
> In the sunny haze of the languid
> (From the Internet)

15. Of course it is notable, as stated before, that the greatest success of Rabindranath Tagore was his beautiful songs / lyrics numbering about 2000, out of which maximum about 200 (two hundred) songs are living with popularity even today.

16. The other songs are no more popular or became the choice of doing research for the advanced scholars, singers and critics engaged in in-depth analysis of *'Rabindrasangeet'* (Tagore-songs).

17. The music, rhythm and rhymes, which are collectively known as *Rabindrasangeet*, are beautiful mixture of the Western music and the traditional songs of Lalon Fakir, D. L. Roy and Atul Prasad Sen etc. of his times. These are especially appreciated by the Bengalees only. In spite of many attempts, the *Rabindra Sangeet* adopted in Hindi and other Indian languages could not become popular.

18. Even after being awarded the Nobel Prize, Rabindranath Tagore visited many Eastern and Western countries where he gave many lectures but it is notable that his popularity was in decline in spite of the fact that his writings comprised of many volumes exceeding the same of other Bengalee writers of high value. He visited China and also Japan. Mr. S.K. Das, a Bangladeshi writer who wrote many articles and books on Rabindranath Tagore, came to my chamber for a discussion and told me with stress that when Rabindranath Tagore visited Japan, he was cordially received. But after hearing his lectures many were not satisfied. When he was leaving Japan none of the Japanese who invited him came to see him off at the time of his departure at the airport. We also know that he did not get appreciations from the Chinese people during his visit.

19. Though he was getting more popularity among the Bengalees under the impact of his getting the Nobel Prize, he could not gain superiority in many forms of literature. For example, he could not compose an epic like *Meghnad Badh Kavya* of Michael Madhusudan Datta or compose a notable pastoral poem like *Nakshikanthar Maath* of Jashimuddin or a bold revolutionary poem like *Agnibina* of Kazi Nazrul Islam. These mentioned works are all Bengali publications and by the Bengalee authors.

20. Yes, due to various political, social and traditional reasons, unlike any other writers of the region, Rabindranath Tagore was too much propagated and publicized, both at private level and also at the Governmental level (for example, by the Government of India, the Government of Bangladesh, and the Government of West Bengal at home and through various Missions around

the world). These wide publicity and over projections virtually made him a sacrilege to many of his fans. I do not know of any such huge public patronage and publicity for any author in any other countries of the world. Perhaps none can find any.

21. There were several other poets outside Bengal in British India who composed poetry of much high value. The name of the Urdu poet Dr. Mohammed Iqbal is worth mentioning here, whose collection of poems in the form of a book named *Baang-e-dara*, was published several years before the publication of the English edition of Rabindranath Tagore's *Gitanjali (Song Offerings)* from London.

———————

Chapter 14

Rabindranath Tagore in the 21st century

1. Rabindranath Tagore died in 1941 achieving great literary success, nationally and internationally. But after his passing away, his popularity gradually declined. Today his reputation is more or less limited among the Bengalees and among the research scholars.

2. His writings are today mostly read in prescribed texts for the students. The Bengalee Hindus more widely read his poems because of universal Hindu religious appeals containing the philosophical and spiritual thoughts drawn from *Vedas, Vedantas* and *Upanishads*; and also because of the influence of *Ramayana* and *Mahabharata* throughout his writings. Many Bengalee Hindus adopt his poems and songs for Hindu religious worships with sacred values.

3. It may be noted that his popularity could not be maintained as the classic standard as those of the great Bengalee writers like Bankim Chandra Chatterjee or Sharat Chandra Chatterjee or Michael Madhusudan Datta.

4. At this stage, I feel that the readers may have a look through the essay by Harold M. Hurwitz on Ezra Pound and Rabindranath Tagore in which he stated how the early appreciations of W. B. Yeats, W. H. Auden and Ezra Pound gradually declined after sometime.

(See: *Ezra Pound and Rabindranath Tagore,* by Harold M. Hurwitz in *The Fortnightly Review,* London; *See also*: http://fortnightlyreview.co.uk/2013/05/ezra-pound-rabindranath-tagore/)

5. Even in India today Tagore's writings are not so much popular as those were during the first two decades after his getting the Nobel Prize in 1913. His poems are not selected in many school text books, outside West Bengal of India and Bangladesh.

6. The international dimensions of his literatures stands sharply declined. Of course, the Government of India has been patronizing with keen interest but the readership response is no more remarkable as was during his life time. It will not be an underestimation of the genius of Rabindranath Tagore. But in reality his name and fame have been declining even in India and Bangladesh where his songs have been adopted as the national anthem. Everybody knows that most of the school students do not know about this great author today in many distant parts of India where he was born and flourished.

7. None can deny that Rabindranath Tagore was an extraordinary genius but his popularity during the last one hundred years rose primarily due to his getting the Nobel Prize rather than the intrinsic values of his writings. Without Nobel Prize, it seems that Rabindranath Tagore never could surpass the popularity of the Bengalee writers like Bankim Chandra Chatterjee or Sharat Chandra Chatterjee in Bengal among the Bengalees.

8. After the death of Rabindranath Tagore in 1941, today the copyright of his publications no more exists exclusively to his own publication house Vishva Bharati. Several editions of his complete works were published from Calcutta of India as well as from Dhaka of Bangladesh. But those new editions of his works could not go into subsequent editions in spite of huge public efforts made by Delhi as well as Dhaka.

9. As such, Rabindranath Tagore, though too much politicized and propagated, could not remain with ascending glory and popularity, even among the Bengali-speaking peoples, like William Shakespeare who lives evergreen to the readers around the world even after about four and a half centuries, without any Nobel Prize. There are hundreds of such examples. But, since he is the "best" in various forms of Bengali literary works, the Bengalees often call him as 'World Poet' (*Vishva Kavi* in Bengali).

10. Yes, Literature and Propaganda (in the form of advertisements, promotions, and forced sales, etc.) are inter-related, but in the long run survival and growing popularity of any literature depend on its intrinsic qualities, universal values and appeals.

Chapter 15

Epilogue

1. It may be noted that the volume of Bengali literature until the end of 19th century was quite small in comparison to those in the European languages.

2. The literary publications increase its volume with the increase of readers. The common readers in the Bengali language have been quite small until the end of World War II, which is before the partition of the British Raj in India in 1947.

3. It is painful to say that even in the 21st century the percentage of the Bengalee readers has not satisfactorily increased when compared with the increasing population. It is sad to note that even after the London planned partition of India in 1947 several decades have passed but the percentage of the Bengalee readers remains same as it was several decades ago.

4. Most of the Bengalees in India and Bangladesh today are not educated enough to read and appreciate literary works. Rabindranath Tagore was born in Calcutta and wrote in Bengali. But even the readers in West Bengal, India are not well educated to grasp the literary genius of Rabindranath Tagore primarily due to low percentage of education. Only the Calcutta readers have been taking interest in his writings and songs. But it must be noted that most of the readers of and writers on Rabindranath Tagore in Calcutta are Hindu Bengalees and of Bangladesh origin. They are from among the migrants from the Bangladesh territory. This difference can be found if anybody studies the

presentations of Tara T.V. Channel of Calcutta. Yes, this Tara T.V. channel is mostly peopled by the migrants from the Bangladesh territory.

5. From the time of British Rule in India, more accurately we may say that after the defeat and killing of Nawab Sirajud Daulah in the Battle of Palassy and thereby occupying Bengal in 1757 to the early 21st century, only a few of the major and notable Bengalee writers emerged. Say, they will not be numbering more than ten. Among them more important and popular are: Bankim Chandra Chatterjee Michael Madhusudan Datta, Rabindranath Tagore, Sharat Chandra Chatterjee, and Kazi Nazrul Islam and a few others. If by any chance and accident these few authors are removed from the library then the Bengali literature will become very poor.

6. None can deny that Rabindranath Tagore greatly enriched the Bengali literature both in quality and in volume. But again it must be admitted by any Bengali reader as to the standard and purity of the writings of Bankim Chandra Chatterjee, though not as a poet and dramatist, stands at the apex of modern Bengali literature.

7. Of course, it gives me great pleasure to add that of late during the last seven decades the Bengali literature has been fast growing. Both in quality and in volume especially due to readership increase in the Bangladesh region.

A Select Bibliography on Rabindranath Tagore

Banerjee, Hiranmay: *Rabindranath Tagore*. 2d ed. New Delhi, Government of India, 1976. One of a series about eminent leaders of India, this biographical narrative presents the depth and diversity of Rabindranath Tagore's character and his contributions to the heritage of India.

Cenkner, William: *The Hindu Personality in Education: Tagore, Gandhi, Aurobindo*. Columbia, Mo., South Asia Books, 1976. Focuses on Tagore's role as the leading Asian educator of the first half of the twentieth century. Surveys his life, thought, and educational theories.

Chakrabarti, Kisor Kumar: *Classical Indian Philosophy of Mind: The Nyāya Dualist Tradition*. Albany, NY: State University of New York Press, 1994.

Chakraverty, Bishweshwar: *Tagore, the Dramatist: A Critical Study*. 4 vols. Delhi, B. R. Publishing, 2000. A scholarly study of Tagore's drama, organized by genre type. Bibliography and index.

Chatterjee, Bhabatosh: *Rabindranath Tagore and Modern Sensibility*. Delhi, Oxford University Press, 1996. This book offers criticism and interpretation of Tagore's work.

Dasgupta, Surendranath: *A History of Indian Philosophy*. 5 Vols. Cambridge, UK: Cambridge University Press, 1922.

Doniger, Wendy: *The Hindus: an Alternative History.* New York Penguin Books, 2009.

Dutta, Krishna, and Andrew Robinson: *Rabindranath Tagore: The Myriad-Minded Man. New York, St. Martin's Press, 1996. This work focuses on the many facets of Tagore.*

Hossain, Md. Asif: *Rabindranath Tagore.* Dhaka, World Book Distribution Centre, 2002. This is a comprehensive, compact and rich source of information on Rabindranath Tagore.

Ivbulis, Viktors: *Tagore: East and West Cultural Unity.* Calcutta, Rabindra Bharati University, 1999. The author looks at the influence of both the West and the East in Tagore's work.

Kripalani, Krishna: *Rabindranath Tagore.* 2d ed. Calcutta, Visva-Bharati, 1980. Written by a scholar well acquainted with the Tagore family, this interesting, 450-page work is considered the best English biography of Tagore.

Lago, Mary M.: *Rabindranath Tagore.* Boston, Twayne, 1976. This literary study concentrates on representative works by Tagore as a lyric poet and writer of short fiction. It suggests a perspective from which to view the national and international response to Tagore's distinguished career.

Mukherjee, Kedar Nath: *Political Philosophy of Rabindranath Tagore.* New Delhi, S. Chand, 1982. In this volume, Mukherjee presents an analysis of Tagore's political philosophy and it emphasizes the value of Tagore's philosophy in contemporary political situations, both in India and the world.

Radhakrishnan, Sarvepalli: *Indian Philosophy.* 2 Vols. London: George Allen & Unwin, 1971.

Thompson, Edward: *Rabindranath Tagore: His Life and Work.* 2d ed. New York, Haskell House, 1974. A reprint of an earlier edition, this brief survey of Tagore's writing prior to 1921 includes commentary based on Thompson's own translations of Tagore's work.

Appendix

[The following complete book of poems entitled: Gitanjali (Song Offerings) by Rabindranath Tagore, is available for a free download and print because its original copyright owned by the Macmillan Company has long expired. The first edition of Gitanjali (Song Offerings) was published in 1912 under the authorship of Rabindranath Tagore and translated into English by himself. Rabindranath Tagore passed away in 1941. As such, the copyright for this collected book of poems, for which the poet Rabindranath Tagore was awarded Nobel Prize for Literature in 1913, does not exist anymore.]

GITANJALI
(SONG OFFERINGS)
BY
RABINDRANATH TAGORE

A collection of prose translations
made by the author from
the original Bengali
with an introduction by
W. B. YEATS
to WILLIAM ROTHENSTEIN

MACMILLAN AND CO., LIMITED
ST. MARTIN'S STREET, LONDON
1913
COPYRIGHT

Formerly issued (1912) in a limited Edition by the India Society
First published by Macmillan & Co. March 1913
Reprinted April, May, June, July (twice), September
October (three times), November (twice), and December (twice) 1913

INTRODUCTION

A few days ago I said to a distinguished Bengali doctor of medicine, 'I know no German, yet if a translation of a German poet had moved me, I would go to the British Museum and find books in English that would tell me something of his life, and of the history of his thought. But though these prose translations from Rabindranath Tagore have stirred my blood as nothing has for years, I shall not know anything of his life, and of the movements of thought that have made them possible, if some Indian traveller will not tell me.' It seemed to him natural that I should be moved, for he said, 'I read Rabindranath every day, to read one line of his is to forget all the troubles of the world.' I said, 'An Englishman living in London in the reign of Richard the Second had he been shown translations from Petrarch or from Dante, would have found no books to answer his questions, but would have questioned some Florentine banker or Lombard merchant as I question you. For all I know, so abundant and simple is this poetry, the new renaissance has been born in your country and I shall never know of it except by hearsay.' He answered, 'We have other poets, but none that are his equal; we call this the epoch of Rabindranath. No poet seems to me as famous in Europe as he is among us. He is as great in music as in poetry, and his songs are sung from the west of India into Burma wherever Bengali is spoken. He was already famous at nineteen when he wrote his first novel; and plays when he was but little older, are still played in Calcutta. I so much admire the completeness of his life; when he was very young he wrote much of natural objects, he would sit all day in his garden; from his twenty-fifth year or so to his thirty-fifth perhaps, when he had a great sorrow, he wrote the most beautiful love poetry in our language'; and then he said with deep emotion, 'words can never express what I owed at seventeen to his love poetry. After that his art grew deeper, it became religious and philosophical; all the inspiration of mankind are in his hymns. He is the first among our saints who

80

has not refused to live, but has spoken out of Life itself, and that is why we give him our love.' I may have changed his well-chosen words in my memory but not his thought. 'A little while ago he was to read divine service in one of our churches---we of the Brahma Samaj use your word 'church' in English---it was the largest in Calcutta and not only was it crowded, but the streets were all but impassable because of the people.'

Other Indians came to see me and their reverence for this man sounded strange in our world, where we hide great and little things under the same veil of obvious comedy and half-serious depreciation. When we were making the cathedrals had we a like reverence for our great men? 'Every morning at three---I know, for I have seen it'---one said to me, 'he sits immovable in contemplation, and for two hours does not awake from his reverie upon the nature of God. His father, the Maha Rishi, would sometimes sit there all through the next day; once, upon a river, he fell into contemplation because of the beauty of the landscape, and the rowers waited for eight hours before they could continue their journey.' He then told me of Mr. Tagore's family and how for generations great men have come out of its cradles. 'Today,' he said, 'there are Gogonendranath and Abanindranath Tagore, who are artists; and Dwijendranath, Rabindranath's brother, who is a great philosopher. The squirrels come from the boughs and climb on to his knees and the birds alight upon his hands.' I notice in these men's thought a sense of visible beauty and meaning as though they held that doctrine of Nietzsche that we must not believe in the moral or intellectual beauty which does not sooner or later impress itself upon physical things. I said, 'In the East you know how to keep a family illustrious. The other day the curator of a museum pointed out to me a little dark-skinned man who was arranging their Chinese prints and said, "That is the hereditary connoisseur of the Mikado, he is the fourteenth of his family to hold the post." 'He answered, 'When Rabindranath was a boy he had all round him in his home literature and music.' I thought of the abundance, of the simplicity of the poems, and said, 'In your country is there much propagandist writing, much criticism? We have to do so much, especially in my own country, that our minds gradually cease to be creative, and yet we cannot help it. If our life was not a continual warfare, we would not have taste, we would not know what is good, we would not find hearers and readers. Four-fifths of our energy is spent in the quarrel with bad taste, whether in our own minds or in the minds of others.' 'I understand,' he replied, 'we too have our propagandist writing. In the villages they recite long mythological poems adapted from the Sanskrit in the Middle Ages, and they often insert passages telling the people that they must do their duties.'

I have carried the manuscript of these translations about with me for days, reading it in railway trains, or on the top of omnibuses and in restaurants, and I have often had to close it lest some stranger would see how much it moved me. These lyrics---which are in the original, my Indians tell me, full of subtlety of rhythm, of untranslatable delicacies of colour, of metrical invention---display in their thought a world I have dreamed of all my live long. The work of a supreme culture, they yet appear as much the growth of the common soil as the grass and the rushes. A tradition, where poetry and religion are the same thing, has passed through the centuries, gathering from learned and unlearned metaphor and emotion, and carried back again to the multitude the thought of the scholar and of the noble. If the civilization of Bengal remains unbroken, if that common mind which---as one divines---runs through all, is not, as with us, broken into a dozen minds that know nothing of each other, something even of what is most subtle in these verses will have come, in a few generations, to the beggar on the roads. When there was but one mind in England, Chaucer wrote his *Troilus and Cressida*, and thought he had written to be read, or to be read out---for our time was coming on apace---he was sung by minstrels for a while. Rabindranath Tagore, like Chaucer's forerunners, writes music for his words, and one understands at every moment that he is so abundant, so spontaneous, so daring in his passion, so full of surprise, because he is doing something which has never seemed strange, unnatural, or in need of defence. These verses will not lie in little well-printed books upon ladies' tables, who turn the pages with indolent hands that they may sigh over a life without meaning, which is yet all they can know of life, or be carried by students at the university to be laid aside when the work of life begins, but, as the generations pass, travellers will hum them on the highway and men rowing upon the rivers. Lovers, while they await one another, shall find, in murmuring them, this love of God a magic gulf wherein their own more bitter passion may bathe and renew its youth. At every moment the heart of this poet flows outward to these without derogation or condescension, for it has known that they will understand; and it has filled itself with the circumstance of their lives. The traveller in the read-brown clothes that he wears that dust may not show upon him, the girl searching in her bed for the petals fallen from the wreath of her royal lover, the servant or the bride awaiting the master's home-coming in the empty house, are images of the heart turning to God. Flowers and rivers, the blowing of conch shells, the heavy rain of the Indian July, or the moods of that heart in union or in separation; and a man sitting in a boat upon a river playing lute, like one of those figures full of mysterious meaning in a Chinese picture, is God Himself. A whole people, a whole civilization, immeasurably strange to us, seems to have been taken up into this imagination; and yet we are not moved because of its strangeness, but because we have met our own image, as though we had walked in Rossetti's willow wood, or heard, perhaps for the first time in literature, our voice as in a dream.

Since the Renaissance the writing of European saints---however familiar their metaphor and the general structure of their thought---has ceased to hold our attention. We know that we must at last forsake the world, and we are accustomed in moments of weariness or exaltation to consider a voluntary forsaking; but how can we, who have read so much poetry, seen so many paintings, listened to so much music, where the cry of the flesh and the cry of the soul seems one, forsake it harshly and rudely? What have we in common with St. Bernard covering his eyes that they may not dwell upon the beauty of the lakes of Switzerland, or with the violent rhetoric of the Book of Revelations? We would, if we might, find, as in this book, words full of courtesy. 'I have got my leave. Bid me farewell, my brothers! I bow to you all and take my departure. Here I give back the keys of my door---and I give up all claims to my house. I only ask for last kind words from you. We were neighbours for long, but I received more than I could give. Now the day has dawned and the lamp that lit my dark corner is out. A summons has come and I am ready for my journey.' And it is our own mood, when it is furthest from 'a Kempis or John of the Cross, that cries, 'And because I love this life, I know I shall love death as well.' Yet it is not only in our thoughts of the parting that this book fathoms all. We had not known that we loved God, hardly it may be that we believed in Him; yet looking backward upon our life we discover, in our exploration of the pathways of woods, in our delight in the lonely places of hills, in that mysterious claim that we have made, unavailingly on the woman that we have loved, the emotion that created this insidious sweetness. 'Entering my heart unbidden even as one of the common crowd, unknown to me, my king, thou didst press the signet of eternity upon many a fleeting moment.' This is no longer the sanctity of the cell and of the scourge; being but a lifting up, as it were, into a greater intensity of the mood of the painter, painting the dust and the sunlight, and we go for a like voice to St. Francis and to William Blake who have seemed so alien in our violent history.

We write long books where no page perhaps has any quality to make writing a pleasure, being confident in some general design, just as we fight and make money and fill our heads with politics---all dull things in the doing---while Mr. Tagore, like the Indian civilization itself, has been content to discover the soul and surrender himself to its spontaneity. He often seems to contrast life with that of those who have loved more after our fashion, and have more seeming weight in the world, and always humbly as though he were only sure his way is best for him: 'Men going home glance at me and smile and fill me with shame. I sit like a beggar maid, drawing my skirt over my face, and when they ask me, what it is I want, I drop my eyes and answer them not.' At another time, remembering how his life had once a different shape, he will say, 'Many an hour I have spent in the strife of the good and the evil, but now it is the pleasure of my playmate of the empty days to draw my heart on to him; and I know not why this sudden call to what useless inconsequence.' An innocence, a simplicity that one does not find elsewhere in literature makes the birds and the leaves seem as near to him as they are near to children, and the changes of the seasons great events as before our thoughts had arisen between them and us. At times I wonder if he has it from the literature of Bengal or from religion, and at other times, remembering the birds alighting on his brother's hands, I find pleasure in thinking it hereditary, a mystery that was growing through the centuries like the courtesy of a Tristan or a Pelanore. Indeed, when he is speaking of children, so much a part of himself this quality seems, one is not certain that he is not also speaking of the saints, 'They build their houses with sand and they play with empty shells. With withered leaves they weave their boats and smilingly float them on the vast deep. Children have their play on the seashore of worlds.

They know not how to swim, they know not how to cast nets. Pearl fishers dive for pearls, merchants sail in their ships, while children gather pebbles and scatter them again. They seek not for hidden treasures; they know not how to cast nets.'

W. B. YEATS

September 1912

[It has been learnt that the copy of the book of poems entitled: Gitanjali (Song Offerings), as submitted to the Swedish Academy, did not contain any numbers or titles of the poems. Later on for the convenience of the readers the poems have been separated by serial numbers only and without giving any titles or dates as found in many Bengali editions. – Ed.]

1

Thou hast made me endless, such is thy pleasure. This frail vessel thou emptiest again and again, and fillest it ever with fresh life.

This little flute of a reed thou hast carried over hills and dales, and hast breathed through it melodies eternally new.

At the immortal touch of thy hands my little heart loses its limits in joy and gives birth to utterance ineffable.

Thy infinite gifts come to me only on these very small hands of mine. Ages pass, and still thou pourest, and still there is room to fill.

2

When thou commandest me to sing it seems that my heart would break with pride; and I look to thy face, and tears come to my eyes.

All that is harsh and dissonant in my life melts into one sweet harmony---and my adoration spreads wings like a glad bird on its flight across the sea.

I know thou takest pleasure in my singing. I know that only as a singer I come before thy presence.

I touch by the edge of the far-spreading wing of my song thy feet which I could never aspire to reach.

Drunk with the joy of singing I forget myself and call thee friend who art my lord.

3

I know not how thou singest, my master! I ever listen in silent amazement.

The light of thy music illumines the world. The life breath of thy music runs from sky to sky. The holy stream of thy music breaks through all stony obstacles and rushes on.

My heart longs to join in thy song, but vainly struggles for a voice. I would speak, but speech breaks not into song, and I cry out baffled. Ah, thou hast made my heart captive in the endless meshes of thy music, my master!

4

Life of my life, I shall ever try to keep my body pure, knowing that thy living touch is upon all my limbs.

I shall ever try to keep all untruths out from my thoughts, knowing that thou art that truth which has kindled the light of reason in my mind.

I shall ever try to drive all evils away from my heart and keep my love in flower, knowing that thou hast thy seat in the inmost shrine of my heart.

And it shall be my endeavour to reveal thee in my actions, knowing it is thy power gives me strength to act.

5

I ask for a moment's indulgence to sit by thy side. The works that I have in hand I will finish afterwards.

Away from the sight of thy face my heart knows no rest nor respite, and my work becomes an endless toil in a shoreless sea of toil.

Today the summer has come at my window with its sighs and murmurs; and the bees are plying their minstrelsy at the court of the flowering grove.

Now it is time to sit quite, face to face with thee, and to sing dedication of live in this silent and overflowing leisure.

6

Pluck this little flower and take it, delay not! I fear lest it droop and drop into the dust.

It may not find a place in thy garland, but honour it with a touch of pain from thy hand and pluck it. I fear lest the day end before I am aware, and the time of offering go by.

Though its colour be not deep and its smell be faint, use this flower in thy service and pluck it while there is time.

7

My song has put off her adornments. She has no pride of dress and decoration. Ornaments would mar our union; they would come between thee and me; their jingling would drown thy whispers.

My poet's vanity dies in shame before thy sight. O master poet, I have sat down at thy feet. Only let me make my life simple and straight, like a flute of reed for thee to fill with music.

8

The child who is decked with prince's robes and who has jewelled chains round his neck loses all pleasure in his play; his dress hampers him at every step.

In fear that it may be frayed, or stained with dust he keeps himself from the world, and is afraid even to move.

Mother, it is no gain, thy bondage of finery, if it keeps one shut off from the healthful dust of the earth, if it rob one of the right of entrance to the great fair of common human life.

9

O Fool, try to carry thyself upon thy own shoulders! O beggar, to come beg at thy own door!

Leave all thy burdens on his hands who can bear all, and never look behind in regret.

Thy desire at once puts out the light from the lamp it touches with its breath. It is unholy---take not thy gifts through its unclean hands. Accept only what is offered by sacred love.

10

Here is thy footstool and there rest thy feet where live the poorest, and lowliest, and lost.

When I try to bow to thee, my obeisance cannot reach down to the depth where thy feet rest among the poorest, and lowliest, and lost.

Pride can never approach to where thou walkest in the clothes of the humble among the poorest, and lowliest, and lost.

My heart can never find its way to where thou keepest company with the companionless among the poorest, the lowliest, and the lost.

11

Leave this chanting and singing and telling of beads! Whom dost thou worship in this lonely dark corner of a temple with doors all shut? Open thine eyes and see thy God is not before thee!

He is there where the tiller is tilling the hard ground and where the path-maker is breaking stones. He is with them in sun and in shower, and his garment is covered with dust. Put of thy holy mantle and even like him come down on the dusty soil!

Deliverance? Where is this deliverance to be found? Our master himself has joyfully taken upon him the bonds of creation; he is bound with us all forever.

Come out of thy meditations and leave aside thy flowers and incense! What harm is there if thy clothes become tattered and stained? Meet him and stand by him in toil and in sweat of thy brow.

12

The time that my journey takes is long and the way of it long.

I came out on the chariot of the first gleam of light, and pursued my voyage through the wildernesses of worlds leaving my track on many a star and planet.

It is the most distant course that comes nearest to thyself, and that training is the most intricate which leads to the utter simplicity of a tune.

The traveller has to knock at every alien door to come to his own, and one has to wander through all the outer worlds to reach the innermost shrine at the end.

My eyes strayed far and wide before I shut them and said 'Here art thou!'

The question and the cry 'Oh, where?' melt into tears of a thousand streams and deluge the world with the flood of the assurance 'I am!'

13

The song that I came to sing remains unsung to this day.

I have spent my days in stringing and in unstringing my instrument.

The time has not come true, the words have not been rightly set; only there is the agony of wishing in my heart.

The blossom has not opened; only the wind is sighing by.

I have not seen his face, nor have I listened to his voice; only I have heard his gentle footsteps from the road before my house.

The livelong day has passed in spreading his seat on the floor; but the lamp has not been lit and I cannot ask him into my house.

I live in the hope of meeting with him; but this meeting is not yet.

14

My desires are many and my cry is pitiful, but ever didst thou save me by hard refusals; and this strong mercy has been wrought into my life through and through.

Day by day thou art making me worthy of the simple, great gifts that thou gavest to me unasked---this sky and the light, this body and the life and the mind---saving me from perils of overmuch desire.

There are times when I languidly linger and times when I awaken and hurry in search of my goal; but cruelly thou hidest thyself from before me.

Day by day thou art making me worthy of thy full acceptance by refusing me ever and anon, saving me from perils of weak, uncertain desire.

15

I am here to sing thee songs. In this hall of thine I have a corner seat.

In thy world I have no work to do; my useless life can only break out in tunes without a purpose.

When the hour strikes for thy silent worship at the dark temple of midnight, command me, my master, to stand before thee to sing.

When in the morning air the golden harp is tuned, honour me, commanding my presence.

16

I have had my invitation to this world's festival, and thus my life has been blessed. My eyes have seen and my ears have heard.

It was my part at this feast to play upon my instrument, and I have done all I could.

Now, I ask, has the time come at last when I may go in
and see thy face and offer thee my silent salutation?

17

I am only waiting for love to give myself up at last into his hands.
That is why it is so late and why I have been guilty of such omissions.

They come with their laws and their codes to bind me fast; but
I evade them ever, for I am only waiting for love to give myself up at
last into his hands.

People blame me and call me heedless; I doubt not they are right
in their blame.

The market day is over and work is all done for the busy. Those
who came to call me in vain have gone back in anger. I am only waiting
for love to give myself up at last into his hands.

18

Clouds heap upon clouds and it darkens. Ah, love, why dost thou
let me wait outside at the door all alone?

In the busy moments of the noontide work I am with the crowd,
but on this dark lonely day it is only for thee that I hope.

If thou showest me not thy face, if thou leavest me wholly aside, I
know not how I am to pass these long, rainy hours.

I keep gazing on the far-away gloom of the sky, and my heart
wanders wailing with the restless wind.

19

If thou speakest not I will fill my heart with thy silence and endure it. I will keep still and wait like the night with starry vigil and its head bent low with patience.

The morning will surely come, the darkness will vanish, and thy voice pour down in golden streams breaking through the sky.

Then thy words will take wing in songs from every one of my birds' nests, and thy melodies will break forth in flowers in all my forest groves.

20

On the day when the lotus bloomed, alas, my mind was straying, and I knew it not. My basket was empty and the flower remained unheeded.

Only now and again a sadness fell upon me, and I started up from my dream and felt a sweet trace of a strange fragrance in the south wind.

That vague sweetness made my heart ache with longing and it seemed to me that is was the eager breath of the summer seeking for its completion.

I knew not then that it was so near, that it was mine, and that this perfect sweetness had blossomed in the depth of my own heart.

21

I must launch out my boat. The languid hours pass by on the shore---Alas for me!
The spring has done its flowering and taken leave. And now with the burden of faded futile flowers I wait and linger.

The waves have become clamorous, and upon the bank in the shady lane the yellow leaves flutter and fall.

What emptiness do you gaze upon! Do you not feel a thrill passing through the air with the notes of the far-away song floating from the other shore?

22

In the deep shadows of the rainy July, with secret steps, thou walkest, silent as night, eluding all watchers.

Today the morning has closed its eyes, heedless of the insistent calls of the loud east wind, and a thick veil has been drawn over the ever-wakeful blue sky.

The woodlands have hushed their songs, and doors are all shut at every house. Thou art the solitary wayfarer in this deserted street. Oh my only friend, my best beloved, the gates are open in my house---do not pass by like a dream.

23

Art thou abroad on this stormy night on thy journey of love, my friend? The sky groans like one in despair.

I have no sleep tonight. Ever and again I open my door and look out on the darkness, my friend!

I can see nothing before me. I wonder where lies thy path!

By what dim shore of the ink-black river, by what far edge of the frowning forest, through what mazy depth of gloom art thou threading thy course to come to me, my friend?

24

If the day is done, if birds sing no more, if the wind has flagged tired, then draw the veil of darkness thick upon me, even as thou hast wrapt the earth with the coverlet of sleep and tenderly closed the petals of the drooping lotus at dusk.

From the traveller, whose sack of provisions is empty before the voyage is ended, whose garment is torn and dustladen, whose strength is exhausted, remove shame and poverty, and renew his life like a flower under the cover of thy kindly night.

25

In the night of weariness let me give myself up to sleep without struggle, resting my trust upon thee.

Let me not force my flagging spirit into a poor preparation for thy worship.

It is thou who drawest the veil of night upon the tired eyes of the day to renew its sight in a fresher gladness of awakening.

26

He came and sat by my side but I woke not. What a cursed sleep it was, O miserable me!

He came when the night was still; he had his harp in his hands, and my dreams became resonant with its melodies.

Alas, why are my nights all thus lost? Ah, why do I ever miss his sight whose breath touches my sleep?

27

Light, oh where is the light? Kindle it with the burning fire of desire!

There is the lamp but never a flicker of a flame---is such thy fate, my heart? Ah, death were better by far for thee!

Misery knocks at thy door, and her message is that thy lord is wakeful, and he calls thee to the love-tryst through the darkness of night.

The sky is overcast with clouds and the rain is ceaseless. I know not what this is that stirs in me---I know not its meaning.

A moment's flash of lightning drags down a deeper gloom on my sight, and my heart gropes for the path to where the music of the night calls me.

Light, oh where is the light! Kindle it with the burning fire of desire! It thunders and the wind rushes screaming through the void. The night is black as a black stone. Let not the hours pass by in the dark. Kindle the lamp of love with thy life.

28

Obstinate are the trammels, but my heart aches when I try to break them.

Freedom is all I want, but to hope for it I feel ashamed.

I am certain that priceless wealth is in thee, and that thou art my best friend, but I have not the heart to sweep away the tinsel that fills my room.

The shroud that covers me is a shroud of dust and death; I hate it, yet hug it in love.

My debts are large, my failures great, my shame secret and heavy; yet when I come to ask for my good, I quake in fear lest my prayer be granted.

29

He whom I enclose with my name is weeping in this dungeon. I am ever busy building this wall all around; and as this wall goes up into the sky day by day I lose sight of my true being in its dark shadow.

I take pride in this great wall, and I plaster it with dust and sand lest a least hole should be left in this name; and for all the care I take I lose sight of my true being.

30

I came out alone on my way to my tryst. But who is this that follows me in the silent dark?

I move aside to avoid his presence but I escape him not.

He makes the dust rise from the earth with his swagger; he adds his loud voice to every word that I utter.

He is my own little self, my lord, he knows no shame; but I am ashamed to come to thy door in his company.

31

Prisoner, tell me, who was it that bound you?'

'It was my master,' said the prisoner. 'I thought I could outdo everybody in the world in wealth and power, and I amassed in my own treasure-hose the money due to my king. When sleep overcame me I lay upon the bad that was for my lord, and on waking up I found I was a prisoner in my own treasure-house.'

'Prisoner, tell me, who was it that wrought this unbreakable chain?'

'It was I,' said the prisoner, 'who forged this chain very carefully. I thought my invincible power would hold the world captive leaving me in a freedom undisturbed. Thus night and day I worked at the chain with huge fires and cruel hard strokes. When at last the work was done and the links were complete and unbreakable, I found that it held me in its grip.'

32

By all means they try to hold me secure who love me in this world. But it is otherwise with thy love which is greater than theirs, and thou keepest me free.

Lest I forget them they never venture to leave me alone. But day passes by after day and thou art not seen.

If I call not thee in my prayers, if I keep not thee in my heart, thy love for me still waits for my love.

33

When it was day they came into my house and said, 'We shall only take the smallest room here.'

They said, 'We shall help you in the worship of your God and humbly accept only our own share in his grace'; and then they took their seat in a corner and they sat quiet and meek.

But in the darkness of night I find they break into my sacred shrine, strong and turbulent, and snatch with unholy greed the offerings from God's altar.

34

Let only that little be left of me whereby I may name thee my all.

Let only that little be left of my will whereby I may feel thee on every side, and come to thee in everything, and offer to thee my love every moment.

Let only that little be left of me whereby I may never hide thee.

Let only that little of my fetters be left whereby I am bound with thy will, and thy purpose is carried out in my life---and that is the fetter of thy love.

35

Where the mind is without fear and the head is held high; Where knowledge is free;

Where the world has not been broken up into fragments by narrow domestic walls;

Where words come out from the depth of truth;

Where tireless striving stretches its arms towards perfection;

Where the clear stream of reason has not lost its way into the dreary desert sand of dead habit;

Where the mind is led forward by thee into ever-widening thought and action--- Into that heaven of freedom, my Father, let my country awake.

36

This is my prayer to thee, my lord---strike, strike at the root of penury in my heart.
Give me the strength lightly to bear my joys and sorrows.

Give me the strength to make my love fruitful in service.

Give me the strength never to disown the poor or bend my knees before insolent might.

Give me the strength to raise my mind high above daily trifles. And give me the strength to surrender my strength to thy will with love.

37

I thought that my voyage had come to its end at the last limit of my power,---that the path before me was closed, that provisions were exhausted and the time come to take shelter in a silent obscurity.

But I find that thy will knows no end in me. And when old words die out on the tongue, new melodies break forth from the heart; and where the old tracks are lost, new country is revealed with its wonders.

38

That I want thee, only thee---let my heart repeat without end. All desires that distract me, day and night, are false and empty to the core.

As the night keeps hidden in its gloom the petition for light, even thus in the depth of my unconsciousness rings the cry---'I want thee, only thee'.

As the storm still seeks its end in peace when it strikes against peace with all its might, even thus my rebellion strikes against thy love and still its cry is---'I want thee, only thee'.

39

When the heart is hard and parched up, come upon me with a shower of mercy.

When grace is lost from life, come with a burst of song.

When tumultuous work raises its din on all sides shutting me out from beyond, come to me, my lord of silence, with thy peace and rest.

When my beggarly heart sits crouched, shut up in a corner, break open the door, my king, and come with the ceremony of a king.

When desire blinds the mind with delusion and dust, O thou holy one, thou wakeful, come with thy light and thy thunder.

40

The rain has held back for days and days, my God, in my arid heart. The horizon is fiercely naked---not the thinnest cover of a soft cloud, not the vaguest hint of a distant cool shower.

Send thy angry storm, dark with death, if it is thy wish, and with lashes of lightning startle the sky from end to end.

But call back, my lord, call back this pervading silent heat, still and keen and cruel, burning the heart with dire despair.

Let the cloud of grace bend low from above like the tearful look of the mother on the day of the father's wrath.

41

Where dost thou stand behind them all, my lover, hiding thyself in the shadows? They push thee and pass thee by on the dusty road, taking thee for naught. I wait here weary hours spreading my offerings for thee, while passers-by come and take my flowers, one by one, and my basket is nearly empty.

The morning time is past, and the noon. In the shade of evening my eyes are drowsy with sleep. Men going home glance at me and smile and fill me with shame. I sit like a beggar maid, drawing my skirt over my face, and when they ask me, what it is I want, I drop my eyes and answer them not.

Oh, how, indeed, could I tell them that for thee I wait, and that thou hast promised to come. How could I utter for shame that I keep for my dowry this poverty. Ah, I hug this pride in the secret of my heart.

I sit on the grass and gaze upon the sky and dream of the sudden splendour of thy coming---all the lights ablaze, golden pennons flying over thy car, and they at the roadside standing agape, when they see thee come down from thy seat to raise me from the dust, and set at thy side this ragged beggar girl a-tremble with shame and pride, like a creeper in a summer breeze.

But time glides on and still no sound of the wheels of thy chariot. Many a procession passes by with noise and shouts and glamour of glory. Is it only thou who wouldst stand in the shadow silent and behind them all? And only I who would wait and weep and wear out my heart in vain longing?

42

Early in the day it was whispered that we should sail in a boat, only thou and I, and never a soul in the world would know of this our pilgrimage to no country and to no end.

In that shoreless ocean, at thy silently listening smile my songs would swell in melodies, free as waves, free from all bondage of words.

Is the time not come yet? Are there works still to do? Lo, the evening has come down upon the shore and in the fading light the seabirds come flying to their nests.

Who knows when the chains will be off, and the boat, like the last glimmer of sunset, vanish into the night?

43

The day was when I did not keep myself in readiness for thee; and entering my heart unbidden even as one of the common crowd, unknown to me, my king, thou didst press the signet of eternity upon many a fleeting moment of my life.

And today when by chance I light upon them and see thy signature, I find they have lain scattered in the dust mixed with the memory of joys and sorrows of my trivial days forgotten.

Thou didst not turn in contempt from my childish play among dust, and the steps that I heard in my playroom are the same that are echoing from star to star.

44

This is my delight, thus to wait and watch at the wayside where shadow chases light and the rain comes in the wake of the summer.

Messengers, with tidings from unknown skies, greet me and speed along the road. My heart is glad within, and the breath of the passing breeze is sweet.

From dawn till dusk I sit here before my door, and I know that of a sudden the happy moment will arrive when I shall see.

In the meanwhile I smile and I sing all alone. In the meanwhile the air is filling with the perfume of promise.

45

Have you not heard his silent steps? He comes, comes, ever comes.

Every moment and every age, every day and every night he comes, comes, ever comes.

Many a song have I sung in many a mood of mind, but all their notes have always proclaimed, 'He comes, comes, ever comes.'

In the fragrant days of sunny April through the forest path he comes, comes, ever comes.

In the rainy gloom of July nights on the thundering chariot of clouds he comes, comes, ever comes.

In sorrow after sorrow it is his steps that press upon my heart, and it is the golden touch of his feet that makes my joy to shine.

46

I know not from what distant time thou art ever coming nearer to meet me. Thy sun and stars can never keep thee hidden from me for aye.

In many a morning and eve thy footsteps have been heard and thy messenger has come within my heart and called me in secret.

I know not only why today my life is all astir, and a feeling of tremulous joy is passing through my heart.

It is as if the time were come to wind up my work, and I feel in the air a faint smell of thy sweet presence.

47

The night is nearly spent waiting for him in vain. I fear lest in the morning he suddenly come to my door when I have fallen asleep wearied out. Oh friends, leave the way open to him---forbid him not.

If the sounds of his steps do not wake me, do not try to rouse me, I pray. I wish not to be called from my sleep by the clamorous choir of birds, by the riot of wind at the festival of morning light.

Let me sleep undisturbed even if my lord comes of a sudden to my door.

Ah, my sleep, precious sleep, which only waits for his touch to vanish. Ah, my closed eyes that would open their lids only to the light of his smile when he stands before me like a dream emerging from darkness of sleep.

Let him appear before my sight as the first of all lights and all forms. The first thrill of joy to my awakened soul let it come from his glance. And let my return to myself be immediate return to him.

48

The morning sea of silence broke into ripples of bird songs; and the flowers were all merry by the roadside; and the wealth of gold was scattered through the rift of the clouds while we busily went on our way and paid no heed.

We sang no glad songs nor played; we went not to the village for barter; we spoke not a word nor smiled; we lingered not on the way. We quickened our pave more and more as the time sped by.

The sun rose to the mid sky and doves cooed in the shade. Withered leaves danced and whirled in the hot air of noon. The shepherd boy drowsed and dreamed in the shadow of the banyan tree, and I laid myself down by the water and stretched my tired limbs on the grass.

My companions laughed at me in scorn; they held their heads high and hurried on; they never looked back nor rested; they vanished in the distant blue haze.

They crossed many meadows and hills, and passed through strange, far-away countries. All honour to you, heroic host of the interminable path! Mockery and reproach pricked me to rise, but found no response in me. I gave myself up for lost in the depth of a glad humiliation---in the shadow of a dim delight.

The repose of the sun-embroidered green gloom slowly spread over my heart. I forgot for what I had travelled, and I surrendered my mind without struggle to the maze of shadows and songs.

At last, when I woke from my slumber and opened my eyes, I saw thee standing by me, flooding my sleep with thy smile. How I had feared that the path was long and wearisome, and the struggle to reach thee was hard!

49

You came down from your throne and stood at my cottage door.

I was singing all alone in a corner, and the melody caught your ear. You came down and stood at my cottage door.

Masters are many in your hall, and songs are sung there at all hours. But the simple carol of this novice struck at your love. One plaintive little strain mingled with the great music of the world, and with a flower for a prize you came down and stopped at my cottage door.

50

I had gone a-begging from door to door in the village path, when thy golden chariot appeared in the distance like a gorgeous dream and I wondered who was this King of all kings!

My hopes rose high and me thought my evil days were at an end, and I stood waiting for alms to be given unasked and for wealth scattered on all sides in the dust.

The chariot stopped where I stood. Thy glance fell on me and thou camest down with a smile. I felt that the luck of my life had come at last. Then of a sudden thou didst hold out thy right hand and say 'What hast thou to give to me?'

Ah, what a kingly jest was it to open thy palm to a beggar to beg! I was confused and stood undecided, and then from my wallet I slowly took out the least little grain of corn and gave it to thee.

But how great my surprise when at the day's end I emptied my bag on the floor to find a least little grain of gold among the poor heap. I bitterly wept and wished that I had had the heart to give thee my all.

51

The night darkened. Our day's works had been done. We thought that the last guest had arrived for the night and the doors in the village were all shut. Only some said the king was to come. We laughed and said 'No, it cannot be!'

It seemed there were knocks at the door and we said it was nothing but the wind. We put out the lamps and lay down to sleep. Only some said, 'It is the messenger!' We laughed and said 'No, it must be the wind!'

There came a sound in the dead of the night. We sleepily thought it was the distant thunder. The earth shook, the walls rocked, and it troubled us in our sleep. Only some said it was the sound of wheels. We said in a drowsy murmur, 'No, it must be the rumbling of clouds!'

The night was still dark when the drum sounded. The voice came 'Wake up! delay not!' We pressed our hands on our hearts and shuddered with fear. Some said, 'Lo, there is the king's flag!' We stood up on our feet and cried 'There is no time for delay!'

The king has come---but where are lights, where are wreaths? Where is the throne to seat him? Oh, shame! Oh utter shame! Where is the hall, the decorations? Someone has said, 'Vain is this cry! Greet him with empty hands, lead him into thy rooms all bare!'

Open the doors, let the conch-shells be sounded! in the depth of the night has come the king of our dark, dreary house. The thunder roars in the sky. The darkness shudders with lightning.

Bring out thy tattered piece of mat and spread it in the courtyard. With the storm has come of a sudden our king of the fearful night.

52

I thought I should ask of thee---but I dared not---the rose wreath thou hadst on thy neck. Thus I waited for the morning, when thou didst depart, to find a few fragments on the bed. And like a beggar I searched in the dawn only for a stray petal or two.

Ah me, what is it I find? What token left of thy love? It is no flower, no spices, no vase of perfumed water. It is thy mighty sword, flashing as a flame, heavy as a bolt of thunder. The young light of morning comes through the window and spread itself upon thy bed. The morning bird twitters and asks, 'Woman, what hast thou got?' No, it is no flower, nor spices, nor vase of perfumed water---it is thy dreadful sword.

I sit and muse in wonder, what gift is this of thine. I can find no place to hide it. I am ashamed to wear it, frail as I am, and it hurts me when press it to my bosom. Yet shall I bear in my heart this honour of the burden of pain, this gift of thine.

From now there shall be no fear left for me in this world, and thou shalt be victorious in all my strife. Thou hast left death for my companion and I shall crown him with my life. Thy sword is with me to cut asunder my bonds, and there shall be no fear left for me in the world.

From now I leave off all petty decorations. Lord of my heart, no more shall there be for me waiting and weeping in corners, no more coyness and sweetness of demeanour. Thou hast given me thy sword for adornment. No more doll's decorations for me!

53

Beautiful is thy wristlet, decked with stars and cunningly wrought in myriad-coloured jewels. But more beautiful to me thy sword with its curve of lightning like the outspread wings of the divine bird of Vishnu, perfectly poised in the angry red light of the sunset.

It quivers like the one last response of life in ecstasy of pain at the final stroke of death; it shines like the pure flame of being burning up earthly sense with one fierce flash.

Beautiful is thy wristlet, decked with starry gems; but thy sword, O lord of thunder, is wrought with uttermost beauty, terrible to behold or think of.

54

I asked nothing from thee; I uttered not my name to thine ear. When thou took'st thy leave I stood silent. I was alone by the well where the shadow of the tree fell aslant, and the women had gone home with their brown earthen pitchers full to the brim. They called me and shouted, 'Come with us, the morning is wearing on to noon.' But I languidly lingered awhile lost in the midst of vague musings.

I heard not thy steps as thou camest. Thine eyes were sad when they fell on me; thy voice was tired as thou spokest low---'Ah, I am a thirsty traveller.' I started up from my day-dreams and poured water from my jar on thy joined palms. The leaves rustled overhead; the cuckoo sang from the unseen dark, and perfume of *babla* flowers came from the bend of the road.

I stood speechless with shame when my name thou didst ask. Indeed, what had I done for thee to keep me in remembrance? But the memory that I could give water to thee to allay thy thirst will cling to my heart and enfold it in sweetness. The morning hour is late, the bird sings in weary notes, *neem* leaves rustle overhead and I sit and think and think.

55

Languor is upon your heart and the slumber is still on your eyes.

Has not the word come to you that the flower is reigning in splendour among thorns? Wake, oh awaken! let not the time pass in vain!

At the end of the stony path, in the country of virgin solitude, my friend is sitting all alone. Deceive him not. Wake, oh awaken!

What if the sky pants and trembles with the heat of the midday sun---what if the burning sand spreads its mantle of thirst---

Is there no joy in the deep of your heart? At every footfall of yours, will not the harp of the road break out in sweet music of pain?

56

Thus it is that thy joy in me is so full. Thus it is that thou hast come down to me. O thou lord of all heavens, where would be thy love if I were not?

Thou hast taken me as thy partner of all this wealth. In my heart is the endless play of thy delight. In my life thy will is ever taking shape.

And for this, thou who art the King of kings hast decked thyself in beauty to captivate my heart. And for this thy love loses itself in the love of thy lover, and there art thou seen in the perfect union of two.

57

Light, my light, the world-filling light, the eye-kissing light, heart-sweetening light!

Ah, the light dances, my darling, at the centre of my life; the light strikes, my darling, the chords of my love; the sky opens, the wind runs wild, laughter passes over the earth.

The butterflies spread their sails on the sea of light. Lilies and jasmines surge up on the crest of the waves of light.

The light is shattered into gold on every cloud, my darling, and it scatters gems in profusion.

Mirth spreads from leaf to leaf, my darling, and gladness without measure. The heaven's river has drowned its banks and the flood of joy is abroad.

58

Let all the strains of joy mingle in my last song---the joy that makes the earth flow over in the riotous excess of the grass, the joy that sets the twin brothers, life and death, dancing over the wide world, the joy that sweeps in with the tempest, shaking and waking all life with laughter, the joy that sits still with its tears on the open red lotus of pain, and the joy that throws everything it has upon the dust, and knows not a word.

59

Yes, I know, this is nothing but thy love, O beloved of my heart---this golden light that dances upon the leaves, these idle clouds sailing across the sky, this passing breeze leaving its coolness upon my forehead.

The morning light has flooded my eyes---this is thy message to my heart. Thy face is bent from above, thy eyes look down on my eyes, and my heart has touched thy feet.

60

On the seashore of endless worlds children meet. The infinite sky is motionless overhead and the restless water is boisterous. On the seashore of endless worlds the children meet with shouts and dances.

They build their houses with sand and they play with empty shells. With withered leaves they weave their boats and smilingly float them on the vast deep. Children have their play on the seashore of worlds.

They know not how to swim, they know not how to cast nets. Pearl fishers dive for pearls, merchants sail in their ships, while children gather pebbles and scatter them again. they seek not for hidden treasures, they know not how to cast nets.

The sea surges up with laughter and pale gleams the smile of the sea beach. Death-dealing waves sing meaningless ballads to the children, even like a mother while rocking her baby's cradle. The sea plays with children, and pale gleams the smile of the sea beach.

On the seashore of endless worlds children meet. Tempest roams in the pathless sky, ships get wrecked in the trackless water, death is abroad and children play. On the seashore of endless worlds is the great meeting of children.

61

The sleep that flits on baby's eyes---does anybody know from where it comes? Yes, there is a rumour that it has its dwelling where, in the fairy village among shadows of the forest dimly lit with glow-worms, there hang two timid buds of enchantment. From there it comes to kiss baby's eyes.

The smile that flickers on baby's lips when he sleeps---does anybody know where it was born?

Yes, there is a rumour that a young pale beam of a crescent moon touched the edge of a vanishing autumn cloud, and there the smile was first born in the dream of a dew-washed morning--- the smile that flickers on baby's lips when he sleeps.

The sweet, soft freshness that blooms on baby's limbs---does anybody know where it was hidden so long? Yes, when the mother was a young girl it lay pervading her heart in tender and silent mystery of love---the sweet, soft freshness that has bloomed on baby's limbs.

62

When I bring to you coloured toys, my child, I understand why there is such a play of colours on clouds, on water, and why flowers are painted in tints---when I give coloured toys to you, my child.

When I sing to make you dance I truly now why there is music in leaves, and why waves send their chorus of voices to the heart of the listening earth---when I sing to make you dance.

When I bring sweet things to your greedy hands I know why there is honey in the cup of the flowers and why fruits are secretly filled with sweet juice---when I bring sweet things to your greedy hands.

When I kiss your face to make you smile, my darling, I surely understand what pleasure streams from the sky in morning light, and what delight that is that is which the summer breeze brings to my body---when I kiss you to make you smile.

63

Thou hast made me known to friends whom I knew not. Thou hast given me seats in homes not my own. Thou hast brought the distant near and made a brother of the stranger.

I am uneasy at heart when I have to leave my accustomed shelter; I forget that there abides the old in the new, and that there also thou abidest.

Through birth and death, in this world or in others, wherever thou leadest me it is thou, the same, the one companion of my endless life who ever linkest my heart with bonds of joy to the unfamiliar.

When one knows thee, then alien there is none, then no door is shut. Oh, grant me my prayer that I may never lose the bliss of the touch of the one in the play of many.

64

On the slope of the desolate river among tall grasses I asked her, 'Maiden, where do you go shading your lamp with your mantle? My house is all dark and lonesome---lend me your light!' she raised her dark eyes for a moment and looked at my face through the dusk. 'I have come to the river,' she said, 'to float my lamp on the stream when the daylight wanes in the west.' I stood alone among tall grasses and watched the timid flame of her lamp uselessly drifting in the tide.

In the silence of gathering night I asked her, 'Maiden, your lights are all lit---then where do you go with your lamp? My house is all dark and lonesome---lend me your light.' She raised her dark eyes on my face and stood for a moment doubtful. 'I have come,' she said at last, 'to dedicate my lamp to the sky.' I stood and watched her light uselessly burning in the void.

In the moonless gloom of midnight I ask her, 'Maiden, what is your quest, holding the lamp near your heart? My house is all dark and lonesome---lend me your light.' She stopped for a minute and thought and gazed at my face in the dark. 'I have brought my light,' she said, 'to join the carnival of lamps.' I stood and watched her little lamp uselessly lost among lights.

65

What divine drink wouldst thou have, my God, from this overflowing cup of my life?

My poet, is it thy delight to see thy creation through my eyes and to stand at the portals of my ears silently to listen to thine own eternal harmony?

Thy world is weaving words in my mind and thy joy is adding music to them. Thou givest thyself to me in love and then feelest thine own entire sweetness in me.

66

She who ever had remained in the depth of my being, in the twilight of gleams and of glimpses; she who never opened her veils in the morning light, will be my last gift to thee, my God, folded in my final song.

Words have wooed yet failed to win her; persuasion has stretched to her its eager arms in vain.

I have roamed from country to country keeping her in the core of my heart, and around her have risen and fallen the growth and decay of my life.

Over my thoughts and actions, my slumbers and dreams, she reigned yet dwelled alone and apart.
Many a man knocked at my door and asked for her and turned away in despair.

There was none in the world who ever saw her face to face, and she remained in her loneliness waiting for thy recognition.

67

Thou art the sky and thou art the nest as well.

O thou beautiful, there in the nest is thy love that encloses the soul with colours and sounds and odours.

There comes the morning with the golden basket in her right hand bearing the wreath of beauty, silently to crown the earth.

And there comes the evening over the lonely meadows deserted by herds, through trackless paths, carrying cool draughts of peace in her golden pitcher from the western ocean of rest.

But there, where spreads the infinite sky for the soul to take her flight in, reigns the stainless white radiance. There is no day nor night, nor form nor colour, and never, never a word.

68

Thy sunbeam comes upon this earth of mine with arms outstretched and stands at my door the livelong day to carry back to thy feet clouds made of my tears and sighs and songs.

With fond delight thou wrappest about thy starry breast that mantle of misty cloud, turning it into numberless shapes and folds and colouring it with hues everchanging.

It is so light and so fleeting, tender and tearful and dark, that is why thou lovest it, O thou spotless and serene. And that is why it may cover thy awful white light with its pathetic shadows.

69

The same stream of life that runs through my veins night and day runs through the world and dances in rhythmic measures.

It is the same life that shoots in joy through the dust of the earth in numberless blades of grass and breaks into tumultuous waves of leaves and flowers.

It is the same life that is rocked in the ocean-cradle of birth and of death, in ebb and in flow.

I feel my limbs are made glorious by the touch of this world of life. And my pride is from the life-throb of ages dancing in my blood this moment.

70

Is it beyond thee to be glad with the gladness of this rhythm? to be tossed and lost and broken in the whirl of this fearful joy?

All things rush on, they stop not, they look not behind, no power can hold them back, they rush on.

Keeping steps with that restless, rapid music, seasons come dancing and pass away---colours, tunes, and perfumes pour in endless cascades in the abounding joy that scatters and gives up and dies every moment.

71

That I should make much of myself and turn it on all sides, thus casting coloured shadows on thy radiance---such is thy *maya*.

Thou settest a barrier in thine own being and then callest thy severed self in myriad notes. This thy self-separation has taken body in me.

The poignant song is echoed through all the sky in many-coloured tears and smiles, alarms and hopes; waves rise up and sink again, dreams break and form. In me is thy own defeat of self.

This screen that thou hast raised is painted with innumerable figures with the brush of the night and the day. Behind it thy seat is woven in wondrous mysteries of curves, casting away all barren lines of straightness.

The great pageant of thee and me has overspread the sky. With the tune of thee and me all the air is vibrant, and all ages pass with the hiding and seeking of thee and me.

72

He it is, the innermost one, who awakens my being with his deep hidden touches.

He it is who puts his enchantment upon these eyes and joyfully plays on the chords of my heart in varied cadence of pleasure and pain.

He it is who weaves the web of this *maya* in evanescent hues of gold and silver, blue and green, and lets peep out through the folds his feet, at whose touch I forget myself.

Days come and ages pass, and it is ever he who moves my heart in many a name, in many a guise, in many a rapture of joy and of sorrow.

73

Deliverance is not for me in renunciation. I feel the embrace of freedom in a thousand bonds of delight.

Thou ever pourest for me the fresh draught of thy wine of various colours and fragrance, filling this earthen vessel to the brim.

My world will light its hundred different lamps with thy flame and place them before the altar of thy temple.

No, I will never shut the doors of my senses. The delights of sight and hearing and touch will bear thy delight.

Yes, all my illusions will burn into illumination of joy, and all my desires ripen into fruits of love.

74

The day is no more, the shadow is upon the earth. It is time that I go to the stream to fill my pitcher.

The evening air is eager with the sad music of the water. Ah, it calls me out into the dusk. In the lonely lane there is no passer-by, the wind is up, the ripples are rampant in the river.

I know not if I shall come back home. I know not whom I shall chance to meet. There at the fording in the little boat the unknown man plays upon his lute.

75

Thy gifts to us mortals fulfil all our needs and yet run back to thee undiminished.

The river has its everyday work to do and hastens through fields and hamlets; yet its incessant stream winds towards the washing of thy feet.

The flower sweetens the air with its perfume; yet its last service is to offer itself to thee.

Thy worship does not impoverish the world.

From the words of the poet men take what meanings please them; yet their last meaning points to thee.

76

Day after day, O lord of my life, shall I stand before thee face to face. With folded hands, O lord of all worlds, shall I stand before thee face to face.

Under thy great sky in solitude and silence, with humble heart shall I stand before thee face to face.

In this laborious world of thine, tumultuous with toil and with struggle, among hurrying crowds shall I stand before thee face to face?

And when my work shall be done in this world, O King of kings, alone and speechless shall I stand before thee face to face?

77

I know thee as my God and stand apart---I do not know thee as my own and come closer. I know thee as my father and bow before thy feet---I do not grasp thy hand as my friend's.

I stand not where thou comest down and ownest thyself as mine, there to clasp thee to my heart and take thee as my comrade.

Thou art the Brother amongst my brothers, but I heed them not, I divide not my earnings with them, thus sharing my all with thee.

In pleasure and in pain I stand not by the side of men, and thus stand by thee. I shrink to give up my life, and thus do not plunge into the great waters of life.

78

When the creation was new and all the stars shone in their first splendour, the gods held their assembly in the sky and sang 'Oh, the picture of perfection! the joy unalloyed!'

But one cried of a sudden---'It seems that somewhere there is a break in the chain of light and one of the stars has been lost.'

The golden string of their harp snapped, their song stopped, and they cried in dismay---'Yes, that lost star was the best, she was the glory of all heavens!'

From that day the search is unceasing for her, and the cry goes on from one to the other that in her the world has lost its one joy!

Only in the deepest silence of night the stars smile and whisper among themselves---'Vain is this seeking! unbroken perfection is over all!'

79

If it is not my portion to meet thee in this life then let me ever feel that I have missed thy sight---let me not forget for a moment, let me carry the pangs of this sorrow in my dreams and in my wakeful hours.

As my days pass in the crowded market of this world and my hands grow full with the daily profits, let me ever feel that I have gained nothing---let me not forget for a moment, let me carry the pangs of this sorrow in my dreams and in my wakeful hours.

When I sit by the roadside, tired and panting, when I spread my bed low in the dust, let me ever feel that the long journey is still before me---let me not forget a moment, let me carry the pangs of this sorrow in my dreams and in my wakeful hours.

When my rooms have been decked out and the flutes sound and the laughter there is loud, let me ever feel that I have not invited thee to my house---let me not forget for a moment, let me carry the pangs of this sorrow in my dreams and in my wakeful hours.

80

I am like a remnant of a cloud of autumn uselessly roaming in the sky, O my sun ever-glorious! Thy touch has not yet melted my vapour, making me one with thy light, and thus I count months and years separated from thee.

If this be thy wish and if this be thy play, then take this fleeting emptiness of mine, paint it with colours, gild it with gold, float it on the wanton wind and spread it in varied wonders.

And again when it shall be thy wish to end this play at night, I shall melt and vanish away in the dark, or it may be in a smile of the white morning, in a coolness of purity transparent.

81

On many an idle day have I grieved over lost time. But it is never lost, my lord. Thou hast taken every moment of my life in thine own hands.

Hidden in the heart of things thou art nourishing seeds into sprouts, buds into blossoms, and ripening flowers into fruitfulness.

I was tired and sleeping on my idle bed and imagined all work had ceased.

In the morning I woke up and found my garden full with wonders of flowers.

82

Time is endless in thy hands, my lord. There is none to count thy minutes. Days and nights pass and ages bloom and fade like flowers. Thou knowest how to wait.

Thy centuries follow each other perfecting a small wild flower.

We have no time to lose, and having no time we must scramble for a chances. We are too poor to be late.

And thus it is that time goes by while I give it to every querulous man who claims it, and thine altar is empty of all offerings to the last.

At the end of the day I hasten in fear lest thy gate to be shut; but I find that yet there is time.

83

Mother, I shall weave a chain of pearls for thy neck with my tears of sorrow.

The stars have wrought their anklets of light to deck thy feet, but mine will hang upon thy breast.

Wealth and fame come from thee and it is for thee to give or to withhold them. But this my sorrow is absolutely mine own, and when I bring it to thee as my offering thou rewardest me with thy grace.

84

It is the pang of separation that spreads throughout the world and gives birth to shapes innumerable in the infinite sky.

It is this sorrow of separation that gazes in silence all nights from star to star and becomes lyric among rustling leaves in rainy darkness of July.

It is this overspreading pain that deepens into loves and desires, into sufferings and joy in human homes; and this it is that ever melts and flows in songs through my poet's heart.

85

When the warriors came out first from their master's hall, where had they hid their power? Where were their armour and their arms?

They looked poor and helpless, and the arrows were showered upon them on the day they came out from their master's hall.

When the warriors marched back again to their master's hall where did they hide their power?

They had dropped the sword and dropped the bow and the arrow; peace was on their foreheads, and they had left the fruits of their life behind them on the day they marched back again to their master's hall.

86

Death, thy servant, is at my door. He has crossed the unknown sea and brought thy call to my home.

The night is dark and my heart is fearful---yet I will take up the lamp, open my gates and bow to him my welcome. It is thy messenger who stands at my door.

I will worship him with folded hands, and with tears. I will worship him placing at his feet the treasure of my heart.

He will go back with his errand done, leaving a dark shadow on my morning; and in my desolate home only my forlorn self will remain as my last offering to thee.

87

In desperate hope I go and search for her in all the corners of my room; I find her not.

My house is small and what once has gone from it can never be regained.

But infinite is thy mansion, my lord, and seeking her I have to come to thy door.

I stand under the golden canopy of thine evening sky and I lift my eager eyes to thy face.

I have come to the brink of eternity from which nothing can vanish---no hope, no happiness, no vision of a face seen through tears.

Oh, dip my emptied life into that ocean, plunge it into the deepest fullness. Let me for once feel that lost sweet touch in the allness of the universe.

88

Deity of the ruined temple! The broken strings of *Vina* sing no more your praise. The bells in the evening proclaim not your time of worship. The air is still and silent about you.

In your desolate dwelling comes the vagrant spring breeze. It brings the tidings of flowers---the flowers that for your worship are offered no more.

Your worshipper of old wanders ever longing for favour still refused. In the eventide, when fires and shadows mingle with the gloom of dust, he wearily comes back to the ruined temple with hunger in his heart.

Many a festival day comes to you in silence, deity of the ruined temple. Many a night of worship goes away with lamp unlit.

Many new images are built by masters of cunning art and carried to the holy stream of oblivion when their time is come.

Only the deity of the ruined temple remains unworshipped in deathless neglect.

89

No more noisy, loud words from me---such is my master's will. Henceforth I deal in whispers. The speech of my heart will be carried on in murmurings of a song.

Men hasten to the King's market. All the buyers and sellers are there. But I have my untimely leave in the middle of the day, in the thick of work.

Let then the flowers come out in my garden, though it is not their time; and let the midday bees strike up their lazy hum.

Full many an hour have I spent in the strife of the good and the evil, but now it is the pleasure of my playmate of the empty days to draw my heart on to him; and I know not why is this sudden call to what useless inconsequence!

90

On the day when death will knock at thy door what wilt thou offer to him?

Oh, I will set before my guest the full vessel of my life---I will never let him go with empty hands.

All the sweet vintage of all my autumn days and summer nights, all the earnings and gleanings of my busy life will I place before him at the close of my days when death will knock at my door.

91

O thou the last fulfillment of life, Death, my death, come and whisper to me!

Day after day I have kept watch for thee; for thee have I borne the joys and pangs of life.

All that I am, that I have, that I hope and all my love have ever flowed towards thee in depth of secrecy. One final glance from thine eyes and my life will be ever thine own.

The flowers have been woven and the garland is ready for the bridegroom. After the wedding the bride shall leave her home and meet her lord alone in the solitude of night.

92

I know that the day will come when my sight of this earth shall be lost, and life will take its leave in silence, drawing the last curtain over my eyes.

Yet stars will watch at night, and morning rise as before, and hours heave like sea waves casting up pleasures and pains.

When I think of this end of my moments, the barrier of the moments breaks and I see by the light of death thy world with its careless treasures. Rare is its lowliest seat, rare is its meanest of lives.

Things that I longed for in vain and things that I got---let them pass. Let me but truly possess the things that I ever spurned and overlooked.

93

I have got my leave. Bid me farewell, my brothers! I bow to you all and take my departure.

Here I give back the keys of my door---and I give up all claims to my house. I only ask for last kind words from you.

We were neighbours for long, but I received more than I could give. Now the day has dawned and the lamp that lit my dark corner is out. A summons has come and I am ready for my journey.

94

At this time of my parting, wish me good luck, my friends! The sky is flushed with the dawn and my path lies beautiful.

Ask not what I have with me to take there. I start on my journey with empty hands and expectant heart.

I shall put on my wedding garland. Mine is not the red-brown dress of the traveller, and though there are dangers on the way I have no fear in mind.

The evening star will come out when my voyage is done and the plaintive notes of the twilight melodies be struck up from the King's gateway.

95

I was not aware of the moment when I first crossed the threshold of this life.
What was the power that made me open out into this vast mystery like a bud in the forest at midnight!

When in the morning I looked upon the light I felt in a moment that I was no stranger in this world, that the inscrutable without name and form had taken me in its arms in the form of my own mother.

Even so, in death the same unknown will appear as ever known to me. And because I love this life, I know I shall love death as well.

The child cries out when from the right breast the mother takes it away, in the very next moment to find in the left one its consolation.

96

When I go from hence let this be my parting word, that what I have seen is unsurpassable.

I have tasted of the hidden honey of this lotus that expands on the ocean of light, and thus am I blessed---let this be my parting word.

In this playhouse of infinite forms I have had my play and here have I caught sight of him that is formless.

My whole body and my limbs have thrilled with his touch who is beyond touch; and if the end comes here, let it come---let this be my parting word.

97

When my play was with thee I never questioned who thou wert. I knew nor shyness nor fear, my life was boisterous.

In the early morning thou wouldst call me from my sleep like my own comrade and lead me running from glade to glade.

On those days I never cared to know the meaning of songs thou sangest to me. Only my voice took up the tunes, and my heart danced in their cadence.

Now, when the playtime is over, what is this sudden sight that is come upon me? The world with eyes bent upon thy feet stands in awe with all its silent stars.

98

I will deck thee with trophies, garlands of my defeat. It is never in my power to escape unconquered.

I surely know my pride will go to the wall, my life will burst its bonds in exceeding pain, and my empty heart will sob out in music like a hollow reed, and the stone will melt in tears.

I surely know the hundred petals of a lotus will not remain closed for ever and the secret recess of its honey will be bared.

From the blue sky an eye shall gaze upon me and summon me in silence. Nothing will be left for me, nothing whatever, and utter death shall I receive at thy feet.

99

When I give up the helm I know that the time has come for thee to take it. What there is to do will be instantly done. Vain is this struggle.

Then take away your hands and silently put up with your defeat, my heart, and think it your good fortune to sit perfectly still where you are placed.

These my lamps are blown out at every little puff of wind, and trying to light them I forget all else again and again.

But I shall be wise this time and wait in the dark, spreading my mat on the floor; and whenever it is thy pleasure, my lord, come silently and take thy seat here.

100

I dive down into the depth of the ocean of forms, hoping to gain the perfect pearl of the formless.

No more sailing from harbour to harbour with this my weather-beaten boat. The days are long passed when my sport was to be tossed on waves.
And now I am eager to die into the deathless.

Into the audience hall by the fathomless abyss where swells up the music of toneless strings I shall take this harp of my life.

I shall tune it to the notes of forever, and when it has sobbed out its last utterance, lay down my silent harp at the feet of the silent.

101

Ever in my life have I sought thee with my songs. It was they who led me from door to door, and with them have I felt about me, searching and touching my world.

It was my songs that taught me all the lessons I ever learnt; they showed me secret paths, they brought before my sight many a star on the horizon of my heart.

They guided me all the daylong to the mysteries of the country of pleasure and pain, and, at last, to what palace gate have the brought me in the evening at the end of my journey?

102

I boasted among men that I had known you. They see your pictures in all works of mine. They come and ask me, 'Who is he?' I know not how to answer them. I say, 'Indeed, I cannot tell.' They blame me and they go away in scorn. And you sit there smiling.

I put my tales of you into lasting songs. The secret gushes out from my heart. They come and ask me, 'Tell me all your meanings.' I know not how to answer them. I say, 'Ah, who knows what they mean!' They smile and go away in utter scorn. And you sit there smiling.

103

In one salutation to thee, my God, let all my senses spread out and touch this world at thy feet.

Like a rain-cloud of July hung low with its burden of unshed showers let all my mind bend down at thy door in one salutation to thee.

Let all my songs gather together their diverse strains into a single current and flow to a sea of silence in one salutation to thee.

Like a flock of homesick cranes flying night and day back to their mountain nests let all my life take its voyage to its eternal home in one salutation to thee.

Index

This <u>select</u> Key-word Index is provided for the quick reference use to the readers. The first number in the bold type in <u>square brackets</u> refers to the Chapter number and the number in normal type refers to the Paragraph number of the Chapter. All Key-words are with reference to the numbered Paragraphs of the text and not to the quotations and references.

Abraham: [10] 3

Afghanistan: [Preface] 14

Agnibina: [13] 19

Alipore: [4] 8, [7] 3

All India National Congress: [6] 2, [8] 6, 8

All-India Language: [Preface] 3

Anglicans: [7] 7

'Anglo-Indian Poet': [12] 2, [13] 4

Arabic: [4] 2

Arabs: [2] 14

Aryans: [Preface] 12

Assam: [Preface] 23

Auden, W. H.: [11] 14, [13] 12

Ayatollahs, Iranian: [9] 5

Azad, *Maulana* Abul Kalam: [8] 7, 8

Baange Dara: [13] 21

Banerjee, (Dr.) Argha: [12] 11

Banerjee, W. C.: [6] 2

Bangladesh: [Preface] 2, 5, 23

Bangladesh Liberation War: [Preface] 2

Baptists: [7] 7

Baul Songs: [5] 9

Bengal: [5] 5, [8] 3, [14] 7

Bengal, East: [8] 3

Bengal, West: [Preface] 23, [1] 14

Bengalee Brahmin Hindus: [8] 2

Bengalee Hindus: [4] 3, 6, 11, [8]

Bengalee readers: [Preface] 24, [1] 5, 6

Bengalees: [Preface] 7, 23, 24, [4] 14

Bengali: [Preface] 19, 24, 25, [4] 9

Bhagirathi: [2] 7

Bhumiputra: [4] 2

Big Bazar: [7] 8

Bihar: [Preface] 23, [4] 3, 7, [7] 5

Biswas, Kumud: [10] 9

Bombay: [2] 5

Bose, (Dr.) Amalendu: [Preface] 19

Bose, Buddhadev: [Preface] 19

Bose, Khudiram: [6] 3

Bose, *Netaji* Subhas Chandra: [Preface] 4, [8] 9

Bose, Sarat Chandra: [8] 9

Bowbazar: [7] 7

Brahmins: [3] 1

Brahmmo Dharma: [9] 1
Brahmo Samaj: [3] 3, [4] 10, [6] 5, [9] 1
Bristol, U.K.: [3] 4
British Navy: [2] 2, 3
British Raj: [Preface] 8, [2] 4, 13, [4] 2, 11, 12, [6] 2, 5, [8] 6, [10] 6, 7, [11] 7
Britishers: [Preface] 4, 6,
Calcutta: [Preface] 8, 23, 24, [1] 11, [2] 5, [4] 8, [7] 3
Calcutta Madrassah: [3] 4
Calcutta University: [3] 11
Calcutta Muslims: [4] 9
Calcutta Urdu: [4] 9
Carey, William: [3] 5
Central India: [4] 7
Charnok, Job: [2] 5
Chatterjee, Bankim Chandra: [Preface] 16, [4] 4, [14] 3
Chatterjee, Sharat Chandra: [14] 3
China: [13] 18
Chowringee Road: [3] 10
Christian Literature and Culture: [Preface] 17
Christianity: [2] 1, [3] 3, [7] 7, [9] 1
Clive, *Lord* Robert: [Preface] 7
College Street, Calcutta: [3] 11
Colutola, Calcutta: [4] 7
Curzon, Lord: [6] 6, [8] 9
Das, Subrata Kumar: [1] 8, [13] 18
Datta, Michael Madhusudan: [Preface] 16, [4] 4, [13] 19
Daulah, *Nawab* Sirajud: [2] 12, [3] 1, [4] 1, [9] 1
Delhi:[1] 11, [14] 8
Dey, Bishnu: [Preface] 19
Dhaka: [Preface] 2, 24, [1] 11, [14] 8
East India Company: [Preface] 7, [2] 3, 5, 6, 8, 9
Egypt: [10] 4
England: [Preface] 21, [3] 3, 5
Esplanade-BBD Bagh: [7] 4
Faguet, *Professor* Emile: [11] 13

Fort William: [2] 6, [7] 3
French Academy: [11] 13
Gandhi, *Mahatma* M. K.: [6] 2, 6, [8] 6, 7
Ganges: [2] 7
Ghalib, Mirza: [7] 3
Gitanjali: [Preface] 19, [10] 8, [11] 6, 12, [13] 1
Gitanjali ('Song offerings'): [Preface] 19, [4] 12, [10] 8, [11] 6, 12, [13] 1
Goebbels, Joseph: [1] 1
Government of Bangladesh: [13] 20
Government of India: [13] 20
Government of West Bengal: [13] 20
Govindapur: [2] 5
Hjarne, Harald: [12] 2, 8, 9
Hardy, Thomas: [13] 11
Hermelin, Carola: [Preface] 11, [11] 9, 10
Hindi: [Preface] 3, [4] 2
Hindu College: [3] 4
Hindu Focus: [12] 3
Hindus: [Preface] 12, [3] 6
Hitler, Adolf: [1] 1
Homer: [Preface] 13, 15
Hurwitz, Harold M.: [14] 4
India: [Preface] 2, 4, 12
India Society: [11] 6
India Wins Freedom: [8] 7
Iqbal, (Dr.) Muhammad: [13] 21
Islam, Kazi Nazrul: [13] 19
Islamabad: [Preface] 2
Islamic Literature and Culture: [Preface] 17
Istanbul: [2] 1
Janaganamana Adhinayak Jayahey…: [4] 2
Japan: [13] 18
Jasimuddin: [13] 19
Jerusalem Post: [10] 12
Jesus Christ: [10] 3
Jesus Road: [10] 3
Jews: [Preface] 20, 21, [7] 7, [10] 3, 4, 5, 6
Jharkhand: [Preface] 23, [4] 3
Jorasanko: [6] 4, [7] 4

Kalidas: [Preface] 16

Kalighat: [2] 5

Karachi: [Preface] 2

Karnad, Girish: [1] 7, [13] 13

Kashmir: [10] 3

Khidderpore: [4] 8

Lalon Fakir: [5] 2

Macaulay, Thomas Babington: [Preface] 7

Macbeth: [10] 2

Madras: [2] 5

Mahabharata: [Preface] 12, 13, 16, [13] 7

Marsden Street, Calcutta: [7] 3

Mary: [10] 3

Matiaburj, Calcutta: [4] 8, [7] 3

Meghnad Badh Kavya: [13] 19

Mein Kampf: [1] 1

Middle Ages: [2] 1

Middle-East: [Preface] 23

Moore, Thomas Sturge: [11] 8

Moses: [10] 3

Mountbatten, Governor-General *Lord*: [Preface] 1, [8] 7

Mughal Emperor: [2] 3

Mughals: [2] 3, 5

Mukherjee, Shyama Prasad: [8] 9

Murshidabad: [3] 1

Muslim Countries: [2] 14

Muslim Rule: [4] 3

Muslims: [Preface] 2, [2] 10, 14

Mysore: [7] 3

Nakshikanthar Maath: [13] 19

Narkeldanga, Calcutta: [4] 8

National Library of India: [4] 6

Nehru, Jawaharlal: [6] 6, [8] 8

New Delhi: [Preface] 2, 8

Nobel Committee: [Preface] 11, [10] 8, [11] 13, [12] 6

Nobel Prize: [Preface] 11, 20, [1] 3, 5, 9, 14, [4] 12, [14] 7

Nobel, Alfred: [Preface] 20

Non-Bengalees: [3] 1

North India: [4] 7

Orissa: [Preface] 23, [4] 3, [7] 5

Oudh: [7] 4

Pakistan: [Preface] 2, 12, 14

Pakistan, East *(formerly)*: [Preface] 2, 4, 5

Pakistan, West *(formerly)*: [Preface] 2, 5

Palassy, Battle of: [2] 12, 13

Palestinians: [10] 4

Park Circus, Calcutta: [4] 8 [7] 3

Park Street, Calcutta: [7] 7

Patel, Sardar Ballabhbhai: [6] 6, [8] 8

Pathuria Ghata Street, Calcutta: [7] 4

Patterson, Jonna: [11] 9

Permanent Settlement: [3] 2

Persian: [4] 2

Persian literature: [9] 4, 5

Phulbagan, Calcutta: [4] 8

Pound, Ezra: [14] 4

Presidency College, Calcutta: [Preface] 19

Protestants: [7] 7

Puranas: [Preface] 12, [11] 2, [13] 7

'Quit India' movement: [6] 2

Rabindra Sangeet: [Preface] 19

Rahman, *Bangabandhu* Sheikh Mujibur: [Preface] 4

Ramayana: [Preface] 12, 13, 17, [13] 7

Ramkrishna, *Shri*: [3] 6

Ray, Satyajit: [1] 12, 14

Rehov Tagore, Tel Aviv: [10] 14

Ripon Street, Calcutta: [4] 3

Robinson, Andrew: [1] 12

Roman Catholics: [7] 7

Roman Empire: [10] 4

Rothenstein, William: [10] 8

Roy, D. L.: [5] 2

Roy, Kiran Shankar: [8] 9

Roy, Professor (Dr.) Nihar Ranjan: [Preface] 19

Roy, *Raja* Ram Mohan: [Preface] 16, [3] 1, 2, [4] 4

Salomon, Carol: [5] 9

Sanskrit: [4] 5, 12

Sanskrit College: [3] 4

Satyajit Ray: The Inner Eye: [1] 12, 13

Sen, Atul Prasad: [5] 4

Sen, Dinesh Chandra: [1] 5, [13] 7

Sen, (Professor) T. N.: [Preface] 19

Shakespeare, William: [10] 2, [14] 9

Stockholm: [Preface] 11

Suhrawardy, Hussain Shaheed: [8] 9

Sun-Set law: [3] 2

Sutanuti: [2] 5

Sutee: [3] 1

Swedish Academy: [Preface] 11, 21, [11] 9, 12

Tagore, *Prince* Dwarkanath: [2] 7, [3] 1, [4] 2, [7] 2, 4

Tagore, Rabindranath: [Preface] 9, 10, 16, 17, 19, 20, 21, 26, [1] 3, 4, 5 6 7, 9, 11, 12, [4] 2, 12, [14] 6, 7, 8, 9

Taltala (Lane), Calcutta: [4] 8, [7] 3

Tatibagan, Calcutta: [4] 8

Terrorist Movement: [6] 2

The History of Bengali Language and Literature: [1] 5, [13] 7

Tripura: [Preface] 23

Turkey: [2] 1

Turks: [2] 14

United Bengal: [4] 2

United Nations: [8] 9

United States: [Preface] 21, [1] 2

United States Information Service Library, Calcutta: [7] 8

Upanishads: [Preface] 21, [11] 2, [13] 12

Urdu: [Preface] 5, [4] 2

Vedas: [Preface] 12, [11] 2, [13] 12

Vidyasagar, Ishwar Chandra: [Preface] 16, [3] 1, 4, [4] 4

Vishva Bharati: [14] 8

Vivekananda, *Swami*: [3] 6, 7

Wazed Ali Shah: [7] 4

West Asia: [10] 4

Western Christian Priests: [9] 1

Western Literature: [13] 14

Western music: [5] 3

Whitways & Ludlow's, Calcutta: [3] 10, [7] 8

Yeats, W. B.: [10] 8, [11] 6, 14, [13] 12

Zionists: [10] 14

Printed in the United States
By Bookmasters